We Don't Need
Another Hero

We Don't Need Another Hero

Struggle, Hope, and Possibility in the Age of High-Stakes Schooling

Gregory Michie

Foreword by
Sonia Nieto

Teachers College
Columbia University
New York and London

Published by Teachers College Press, 1234 Amsterdam Avenue, New York, NY 10027

"Teaching in the Undertow" originally appeared in somewhat different form in "The New Teacher Book: Finding Purpose, Balance, and Hope During Your First Years in the Classroom" (*Rethinking Schools,* 2004). Reprinted by permission of the author.
"All Together Now" first appeared in *Teacher Magazine* (February 2002). Reprinted by permission of the author.
"From the Trading Floor to the Classroom: Charlie's Story" first appeared in somewhat different form in *Teacher Magazine* (January/February 2005). Reprinted by permission of the author.
"Seeing, Hearing, and Talking Race: Lessons for White Teachers from Teachers of Color" first appeared in *Multicultural Perspectives*, 9(1), 3–9. Reprinted by permission of Taylor & Francis Ltd, http://www.tandf.co.uk/journals.
"Fire and Water: Reflections on Teaching in the City" first appeared in *Burned In: Fueling the Fire to Teach* (2011). Reprinted by permission of Teachers College Press.
"Ground Zero" is excerpted from a collection entitled *Zero Tolerance: Resisting the Drive for Punishment in Our Schools*. Copyright © 2001 by William Ayers, Bernardine Dohrn, and Rick Ayers. Reprinted by permission of The New Press, www.thenewpress.com
"A Real Alternative: Tragedy and Hope on Chicago's South Side" originally appeared in *The International Journal on School Disaffection*, 4(2), 6–13. Reprinted by permission of the National Dropout Prevention Center and Trentham Books.
"Elephants in the Room" originally appeared in somewhat different form in *Rethinking Schools*, 21(3), Spring 2007. Reprinted by permission of the author.
"Another Path is Possible" originally appeared in *Rethinking Schools*, 24(1), Fall 2009. Reprinted by permission of the author.

Library of Congress Cataloging-in-Publication Data can be obtained at www. loc.gov

ISBN 978-0-8077-5350-7 (paperback)

Printed on acid-free paper
Manufactured in the United States of America

19 18 17 16 15 14 13 12   8 7 6 5 4 3 2 1

Contents

Part III: The Bigger Picture

Foreword

Probably because I've spent my professional life in classrooms, first as a teacher and later as a teacher educator, stories about schools and classrooms always appealed to me. But lately I find most school stories stale, uninteresting, and exceedingly predictable: Young idealistic teacher (usually White) begins teaching surly, disrespectful, and angry kids (usually African American and Latino) in a dilapidated urban school, while facing numerous challenges of discipline, motivation, and hostility along the way. Veteran teachers are depicted as jaded, administrators as uncaring, and parents as negligent. Sometimes the "good guys" are charter schools and the "bad guys" are teacher unions, but the "bad guys" can just as easily be other teachers, administrators, teacher educators, or parents. An hour and a half later, at the end of the story or movie, the teacher has become a master at her trade and the students have been transformed into well-behaved, enthusiastic, and motivated young people.

The story line of these made-for-Hollywood tales may differ, but the moral is typically the same: Our public schools are a disgrace except for a few "saviors," whether teachers, philanthropists, or visionary administrators. Most patrons leave the movie theater with warm cozy visions of what can be accomplished, even with "difficult children" living in dire circumstances. Most people, that is, except teachers.

Teachers know that school stories must be about more than spinning a tale, because classrooms and schools are quite a bit more complicated than such movies would have us believe. The real culprits—poverty, racism, institutional neglect, and other structural obstacles to equality and justice—are missed when classrooms, schools, teachers, and students are painted with such broad strokes. In fact, these conditions are mentioned only in passing, if at all, in superficial stories about urban schools.

Greg Michie tells stories, too, but, in contrast, his stories offer not just feel-good accounts or happy endings (although sometimes these happen in spite of brutal school and societal conditions); he also describes the many and constant demands faced by teachers, students, administrators, and families in urban schools and the ways in which caring and intellectually rigorous spaces are created despite the challenges. In honest and realistic fashion, the essays in *We Don't Need Another Hero* offer a cautionary tale about youngsters marginalized by society because of their race, ethnicity, social class, and other differences and who deserve the best we can give them. Underscored throughout these essays is the sociopolitical context of a society that seems to care remarkably little about its most vulnerable youngsters. Through policies, practices, traditions, and ideologies, the more privileged are consistently favored over the less privileged. These include inequitable funding for schools; inadequate professional development for teachers unfamiliar with the reality of their students' lives and communities; meager curricular offerings and low expectations for the most disadvantaged students; little respect for the cultures and languages students bring to school; and few resources for preventing the wholesale dropping out of those who attend schools characterized by violence, gangs, and indifferent educators. Although students do not create these problems, they bear the brunt of the results of such policies.

In *We Don't Need Another Hero,* Greg Michie once again demonstrates why he is so highly regarded as a teacher, teacher educator, and author. In these essays, he turns his critical but loving eye on students, teachers, and schools to illustrate what is wrong with the schools we have today, as well as to help us imagine what schools should be like if they are ever to fulfill our nation's promise of an equal and equitable education for all our students. In these stories, vignettes, and reflections, Michie hits just the right note, rejecting both Pollyanna-like simplistic solutions to the complex problems of our urban schools and the glorification of individual teachers. Instead, as is clear from the title of this powerful book, his vision is one of hope, possibility, and struggle. He not only describes the abysmal conditions in too many schools, but he also provides a cogent analysis of why they have become this way, as well as counterstories that poignantly depict the courage of students, teachers, and administrators who have tried to buck the system.

Michie makes it clear that he believes teachers working collaboratively with administrators, families, and students, although they cannot do it all, can do a great deal to make our schools more humane, compassionate, and creative spaces, particularly for youngsters who have been abandoned by our schools and society. Throughout, he describes visionary teachers and administrators who work tirelessly to help young people live out the American dream of justice and equality. At the same time, because the problems are so immense, their efforts often result in few permanent victories. Given policies such as high-stakes testing mandates and zero-tolerance agendas, Michie makes us wonder how some students manage to succeed at all.

It was hard for me to put this book down. At the same time, it was difficult to read. In spite of my own experience as both a student many years ago, and later, a teacher in crumbling urban schools, the stark inequality described in these pages is difficult to understand. It is so far from our stated ideals of fair play and meritocracy that it should be a call to action for all of us—teachers, students, families, administrators, and, especially, our policymakers—to pour all our resources into changing the situation. How can we allow such conditions to exist and yet insist, with a straight face, that our schools offer all students a fair chance and unlimited opportunities? As Michie suggests, the solutions to these problems are not to be found in more tests or stricter discipline. Rather, it will take the will of the entire nation to turn things around. Yet, given the kind of institutional neglect that students living in poverty have experienced until now, it is hard to see how this might actually happen. I am left both saddened and inspired by these stories.

Yet I am also grateful for the stories told by teachers such as Greg Michie. His vision of hope and possibility in the midst of struggle offers a welcome relief from the brutal stories of "failing schools" and "takeovers," or the saccharine and sanctimonious stories of solitary heroes who turn schools around. He is right: We don't need another hero. The heroes are already there: They are our students, as well as the teachers and administrators who have a passion for justice. Those are the voices we must heed.

Sonia Nieto

Acknowledgments

So much gratitude—

To the teachers, students, school administrators, and others you'll meet in these pages: Charlie Bright; Beto Sepúlveda; Adam Heenan; Nancy Serrano; Liz Kirby; Cynthia Nambo; Toni Billingsley; Juan Palacios; Father Bruce Wellems; Oscar Contreras; Jose Alonso; Brigitte Swenson and the teachers and staff at Dugan Alternative School (now one of the Peace and Education Coalition Alternative High Schools); Tamara Witzl and the teachers and staff at Telpochcalli; Amy Rome and the teachers and staff at NTA; the staff, instructors, and my former students at the Golden Apple Scholars Summer Institute and in the GATE program.

To my friend and former colleague Beth Hatt, who was the brains behind the research project that inspired Chapter 11; and to Sonia Nieto, for generosity beyond measure.

To my amazing colleagues, present and past, especially Isabel Nuñez, Pamela Konkol, Simeon Stumme, Amanda Maddocks, Pete Renn, Carolyn Theard-Griggs, Tom Jandris, Dara Soljaga, Cynthia Grant, Elizabeth Owolabi, Jie Lin, Pauline Clardy, Elizabeth Skinner, Jen O'Malley, Evelyn Perez, Cheryl Witucke, Cesar Nuñez, Simone Alexander, Cristina Pacione-Zayas, and Robert Lee. Extra thanks to Isabel for helpful suggestions on earlier drafts of several chapters.

To Robb Hill and Monique Cruz for the cover photo.

To all the wonderful folks at TC Press: Carole Saltz, Emily Renwick, Dave Strauss, Aureliano Vázquez, Beverly Rivero, and everybody else who helped make this book happen.

Finally, as always, to Lisa and all my family for their love, encouragement, and everday heroics.

Introduction

I had lived in Chicago for nearly 20 years before I paddled down the Chicago River in a canoe for the first time. The river snakes visibly through parts of the city, but until then I'd seen it the way many residents probably see it: glimpses out the window of a car or bus, or distracted glances while hurrying across a bridge downtown. Lots of times, I simply didn't pay much attention to it at all.

But in a canoe, away from the traffic, away from the hulking high-rises of the business district, the river looks and feels different. Paddling along the North Branch, I had to keep reminding myself that I was still in the city. Herons and other birds I couldn't identify peeked out from behind trees. Turtles, one as large as a garbage-can lid, sunned themselves on the muddy banks. I could still hear the familiar rumble of automobiles, but it was muffled, far in the distance, mostly replaced by the rippling of water and a chorus of bird calls. It's a Chicago not many people know well.

The same could be said of the Chicago that exists inside its public school classrooms. While the city's elected officials and power brokers are quick to offer opinions on the state of the schools, few have actually spent significant time inside them, and fewer still have children who attend one. These decision makers may deliver an occasional graduation speech or serve as "principal for a day," but many have little idea of the actual challenges of a teacher's work or the complexities of classroom life. Their views of schools are similar, in many ways, to my early impressions of the river: fleeting, decontextualized, woefully uninformed.

But that doesn't mean their perspectives are ignored. Over the past decade, the debate over public education has been redirected, and even dominated, by people with minimal experience inside schools: business leaders and politicians, rather than educators. While it's hard to imagine turning to "experts" with backgrounds in computer software or health care law if we thought our wetlands or waterways were in peril, we have no qualms about doing so when it comes to our schools. A number of urban systems have hired candidates with no education credentials—an attorney, a magazine executive, a former governor—to head their districts. Billionaire philanthropists Bill Gates and Eli Broad—two more non-educators—have exerted unprecedented influence on federal and state policy through the extended reach of their charitable foundations.[1] And Arne Duncan, who had never been a classroom teacher or school principal before serving as CEO of Chicago Public Schools, was tapped by President Barack Obama to become his education secretary.

Along with the leaders of charter school networks like KIPP and organizations such as Teach for America and Stand for Children, these are the "new reformers" in American education. Together they've engineered not only a fundamental shift toward a business-minded vision of school improvement, but also a shift in the popular narrative about schools. Teachers' unions are the primary villains in this telling, with maverick school leaders like former Washington, D.C. schools' chief Michelle Rhee held up as its heroes. Educators who question the wisdom of the market-driven reforms are cast as "protectors of the status quo," and accused of making "excuses" for poor children rather than pushing them to succeed. Most troubling, the democratic ideal in schools has been replaced by a capitalist playbook, emphasizing competition at every turn: kids for the highest test scores, teachers for bigger "achievement" bonuses, states for federal funding, and the United States in a bid to "win the future."

This change in rhetoric has filtered down to schools as well, where the language we use to talk about teaching and learning has devolved into a bizarre mimicry of corporate-speak. "Strategic kids" are those whose test scores are closest to the required threshold and thus get additional one-on-one instructional support. Charter school planners fret about their "brand identity" and "competitive positioning." Teachers are rated based on their "value-added quotient." And everything—*everything*—must be "data-driven." Instruction—data-driven. Decision-making—data-driven. Photocopier usage—I wouldn't be surprised.

Even in university-based teacher preparation programs, where I spend much of my time these days, the obsession with data has spread like a contagion. Not too long ago I sat in on a meeting with a group of teacher educators who were discussing the possible benefits of adding a more extensive reflective component to their program. "Where's the data?" one professor asked. "I don't make any decision before first combing through a pile of data." I noted later, with some relief, that he did manage to get a second cup of coffee without crunching any numbers first.

But the past ten years have not been all doom and gloom in schools. Teachers, students, parents, and community members have come together in pockets of opposition to the market-driven reforms. Some have pushed back publicly against the idea of schools as test-prep factories: the Save Our Schools march in Washington, D.C. in summer 2011, vocal parent organizations like Parents United for Responsible Education in Chicago, and teacher-bloggers who've exposed the everyday insanity brought about by unwise and unjust policies. Others have worked to create spaces in their own schools and communities that embrace a more democratic, justice-centered vision of education. They understand that, in the words of the Spanish poet Antonio Machado, "*Se hace camino al andar*—We make the road by walking."[2] And even in the face of attacks on teachers' dignity and policies that hinder their work, they keep taking steps, they walk on.

* * *

I wrote the essays and stories in this book over a ten-year period, from 2001 to 2011.[3] While my day job during much of that time was as a university professor, the selections included here reflect the various up-close vantage points I've had in Chicago schools over the years: classroom teacher, school and community volunteer, researcher, and teacher educator in three uniquely structured programs. Some of the chapters have been previously published in magazines, journals, or edited collections; others appear here for the first time. Most of the previously published pieces have been revised for this book, resulting in relatively minor changes for some and extensive rewrites for others. Where appropriate, I've updated statistical information with more recent figures.

Much of what you'll read about here is grounded in Chicago specifically, and in city schools more generally. In part, that's because I myself am grounded there—that's where my own experience has been. But it's also a natural place to begin when considering where we find ourselves as educators in the United States and where we might go from here. Urban schools are in many ways the litmus test for the most critical questions regarding what public education in a democracy should look like: How do we provide a quality, meaningful education to all children—no matter what their street address, or what language they speak at home, or how much money their parents make? How do we provide the kind of education for all children that we desire for our own? Teachers and administrators everywhere struggle to live out answers to these questions; but in urban schools that serve large communities of concentrated poverty, that struggle is all the more immediate, all the more intense, all the more urgent. So, if we want to know how we're doing in terms of educating our most vulnerable children in America, the kids who need good schools most, it makes sense to look first to the cities.

But that doesn't mean the essays and narratives included here speak only to the experiences of urban educators. Far from it—they address issues that reverberate to one degree or another in most U.S. schools. What teacher hasn't struggled to hold on to her values in trying times, or to live out the democratic ideal? Who hasn't wrestled with how to engage marginalized students more authentically, or fought to keep sane amid the madness of high-stakes accountability? From what I've gathered in talks with educators around the country over the past decade, these are concerns that most teachers and school leaders share. But in the data-driven climate in which we live, they're not always given the attention they deserve. My hope is that the pieces I've included here might help spark or rekindle silenced conversations about some of the things that really matter—or should really matter—in schools.

To that end, the accounts in this book are buoyed by a vision of teaching as a humanistic enterprise, of students as multidimensional beings, and of urban schools as spaces where young people can imagine and become, not just "achieve." Part I centers on the classroom, but its focus is not on the compartmentalized mechanics of teachers' work. (One student teacher assessment form I've seen breaks down effective teaching into 117 sub-components.) It's also not concerned with teaching as it's been narrowly redefined in the era of standardization and accountability: good teaching as the delivery of high test scores. Rather, Part I turns its attention to our identities and commitments as teachers: who we are, what we believe in and what we value, how we manage to keep our sights on things that matter within an educational system that values competition, compliance, and control.

Part II focuses on youth who find themselves on the margins of both schools and society. This may not seem like much of a departure from popular education rhetoric, steeped as it is in notions of leaving no children behind. But the light I shine here is not on test-score gaps or statistics, but on young people themselves: their voices, their stories, their analyses of their lives and their futures. The first four pieces in this section form something of a narrative arc, though they were written separately over a span of several years. They center on one of the most reviled groups in popular media accounts of the urban landscape—young men in gangs—and on one community's efforts to re-engage them. The final chapter examines the uncertain path to college facing many low-income Latino and African American students, and the formidable challenges they continue to encounter even once they've "made it" to a predominantly White campus.

In Part III, I turn to the bigger picture—a few of the larger issues that frame the lives and work of urban teachers and their students: the power of popular media representations, the encroachment of federal policies, the impact of the new reformers' "innovations," and the continuing struggle for the democratic ideal in schools. Throughout, my perspective is influenced not only by my experiences in Chicago classrooms, but by a vision of educational equity that borrows from John Rawls' theory of justice.[4] It demands that we begin any discussion of schooling in the United States by asking ourselves: What if any one of us, or our own children, had a real chance of being one of the most disadvantaged members of our society? What kind of schools would we want then?

Most of us would want schools in every community that honor and value our children as they are, that build on their strengths, that provide them with the necessary nurturing and experiences to develop their full human capacity. We'd want schools in every neighborhood with safe and stimulating learning environments, peopled with intellectually curious and caring adults, resourced with well-stocked libraries, and up-to-date teaching tools. We'd want schools that help our kids view the world through multiple lenses, schools that promote justice and the common good. We'd want schools that encourage our children to think deeply and create freely, to imagine and question, schools that see our kids the way we see them: as beautiful, complex, one-of-a-kind, full of wonder and possibility.

* * *

For decades, two distorted storylines have dominated public perceptions about urban schools. The first is one of decay and disorder—"teenage terror in the schools" and "big-city modern savagery," as it was described in the promotional trailer for the 1955 film *Blackboard Jungle*. Competing with this conception has been an equally misleading narrative, that of the individual hero teacher: a sacrificial young idealist who, seemingly overnight, accomplishes the impossible with kids others said couldn't be taught. Think *Freedom Writers* or *The Ron Clark Story*.

More recently, these have been joined, and in many ways eclipsed, by the market-based accountability narrative. It incorporates both of the earlier threads in crafting its updated version of the story: City schools are a mess, and "high-quality" teachers can indeed make a difference, but—the new twist—only with a top-down, data-driven, test-centric approach to teaching and learning. Or, if that fails, by closing down "failing" schools and replacing them with "innovative" charters.

Like the earlier narratives, this latest rendering is deceptive and loaded with half-truths. While it places a welcome focus on supporting students who have been historically ill-served by public schools, it minimizes the importance of outside-school factors, such as family income level or access to resources, that impede the in-school progress of many children. And while it rightly views urban students as potential academic successes, rather than thugs or future dropouts, its fixation on high-stakes testing leaves in its wake a school experience for many low-income students that can only be called impoverished.

We Don't Need Another Hero represents an alternative narrative—one grounded in the relational nature of good teaching, the indomitable spirit of kids on the margins, and the beating heart of urban schools and communities. You won't find piles of data to sift through in these pages, or strategies for raising test scores. But my hope is that you'll find something more powerful: a collage of essays and stories that, in looking closely at teaching and learning in the city, help us better understand the schools we've made, and more vividly imagine those we may yet create.

Part I

Teaching

Chapter 1

Teaching in the Undertow

Resisting the Pull of Schooling-as-Usual

When I was a child, I was amazed by the ocean. I remember being awed as I looked out at the vast expanse of blue-green water off the South Carolina coast. And I recall the cautionary words my mother used each time I tried to wade in deeper than my waist: "Be careful of the undertow," she'd say.

According to my mom, the undertow was an invisible current beneath the ocean's surface that, if you weren't careful, could pull you down the coastline or out to sea before you knew what was happening. It tugged you along almost imperceptibly, she said, so you had to consciously keep your bearings: Pick a recognizable landmark and don't lose sight of it.

I could've used her advice when I began teaching 7th and 8th graders on Chicago's South Side two decades later. I went in with no formal preparation or credentials, and as a White male transplanted from the South, I was an outsider to my students in many ways. My approach at the time grew mostly out of what made sense to me. I thought classrooms should be active spaces where kids had regular opportunities to do and make things. I thought students should be encouraged to creatively express themselves, that their voices should be not only heard, but valued. I believed kids should feel a connection between what they studied in school and their lives outside it, and should be pushed to think critically about the world around them. Most of all, I recognized that a meaningful, quality education was crucial for the young people I would be teaching, whose communities had been largely neglected and abandoned by those in power.

But having beliefs or guiding principles is one thing. Figuring out how to put them into practice, I learned, is another matter altogether, especially if you're teaching at a struggling urban school where the "pedagogy of poverty," as Martin Haberman[1] calls it—characterized by "constant teacher direction and student compliance"—is in widespread use. In that sort of environment, it's easy to lose your footing as a novice teacher, to begin to drift from your anchorage, to be seduced by the pull of convention or expediency or outside demands. The undertow of schooling, you quickly figure out, can be as strong and stealthy as any ocean's. Maybe even more so.

So, how do you resist? The first thing to know is, as much as it may seem otherwise at first, you're not alone. I've spent significant time in dozens of Chicago schools over the years, and while many have their share of adults who have become, at least on the surface, jaded or resigned to mediocrity, I've also found dedicated, caring, even visionary teachers almost everywhere I've been. This is important to understand as a new teacher because it makes it less likely that you'll fall into the trap of seeing yourself as the anointed one, the lone crusader working for justice in an unjust school and world. Heroic teacher memoirs and Hollywood movies notwithstanding, that is rarely, if ever, the way things are.

While the organizational structures and scheduling at your school may not support alliance-building among teachers (and may, in fact, implicitly encourage you to isolate yourself), one of the best things you can do for yourself as a beginning teacher is to seek out allies—both within your school and in the broader community of educators. Fellow teachers with whom you are aligned philosophically and politically can be vital sources of both emotional support and practical ideas, and even those who don't seem to share your views can sometimes prove helpful. A colleague who's been teaching in your building for 25 years, even if "traditional" or "burned out" at first glance, may still have lessons to impart and useful advice to offer, and may, in time, turn out to be not as one-dimensional as you originally thought.

That's not to say that you should expect to be surrounded by hopeful and forward-thinking educators. Cynicism can be deeply entrenched in big-city public schools and also wildly contagious. One of the first temptations for a new teacher is to join this chorus of negativity and begin, however reluctantly, to recite the sorts of excuses you were certain you'd never make: that you can't really get to know your students because there are too many of them, that you can't engage students in group work because they get out of control, that you can't focus on building critical thinking skills when your kids are having a hard enough time just finding a vocabulary word in the dictionary. I've heard myself say or think all those things at one time or another, and they're all legitimate dilemmas.

But Bill Ayers, longtime educator and author of *To Teach*,[2] points out that focusing on all the impediments to your work, while perhaps therapeutic in the short term, is ultimately a dead-end for the committed teacher. Ayers suggests turning each obstacle around and viewing it from a more hopeful perspective by saying, "OK, this is my situation, these are the realities. Given that, what *can* I do?" Maybe you can't do everything you'd planned or imagined—at least not right away—but you can always do something.

It may be that you have to start with something small and seemingly insignificant—like bulletin boards. In many elementary and middle schools, bulletin boards simply become part of the scenery, wallpapered with routine announcements or seasonal messages that rarely provoke thought or cause anyone—adults or kids—to stop and take notice. But bulletin boards can be to teachers and students what blank walls are to graffiti artists: an opportunity—the most visible one of all in many schools—to make a statement, to pose questions, to speak out on an issue, to bring kids' lives into classrooms or hallways. In one school I visited, I saw a bulletin board that featured the words *They were here first* at its center, with the names of a number of American Indian tribes radiating around the outer edges. At another school, 7th-graders recognized the Day of the Dead by displaying letters they'd written to loved ones who had passed away. Still another teacher put up a thought-provoking quote along with an invitation for students to attach quotes they found challenging or inspiring.

Those may not sound like such radical acts when placed alongside the more elaborate proposals of education's critical theorists. But once you're in a classroom of your own, you begin to realize that it's in the details, as much as in the big-picture theorizing, that critical conceptions of teaching find life. Kids can learn about equity and justice from the way community is formed in a classroom, how decisions are made, who is represented on the walls and bookshelves, what sorts of interactions are encouraged and discouraged, whose thoughts and ideas are valued, and, yes, even what's on the bulletin boards. Teaching for social justice, in practice, is as much about the environment you create as it is about the explicit lessons you teach.

Content does matter, though, and it's another area in which, as a new teacher, you'll be challenged to hold true to your beliefs. For one thing, it's likely that you'll feel the ominous cloud of high-stakes testing looming over every curricular decision you make. One of the many tragic consequences of this is that the basic curriculum question—What knowledge and experiences are most worthwhile for my students?—can seem either beyond your purview as a teacher or entirely moot. When you're handed a booklet of state goals or district guidelines, loaded down with textbooks and teachers' guides, and told what sequence of lessons to follow, it's easy for curriculum to become not something you wrestle with or debate, but something you unwrap: a social studies series called "Discoveries," let's say, that gives kids few opportunities and little inspiration to actually make any.

Beyond that, you may be further overwhelmed by all you need to do to make what you teach more meaningful and to lend it a critical perspective: limiting the use of biased and oversimplified textbooks, bringing in primary source documents, connecting topics to real-world issues, reading whole novels instead of chopped-up basal selections, giving students opportunities to write about their lives, weaving the arts throughout your subject areas, inviting your kids to help decide what they want to study, and so on. The enormity of the challenge can be truly paralyzing: because you can't do everything, you delay doing anything, and instead fall back on using textbooks and following directives until you get your feet more firmly on the ground.

But the ground is always shifting when you're a teacher, so your feet may never be fully planted. Instead of waiting for that to happen, take on something more manageable: Start with one subject and commit yourself to bringing it to life for your students, even if you're temporarily relying on canned curricula for other subjects. Or, if you teach only one or two subjects to several groups of kids, try putting your own spin on things one day a week, and then build from there. Again, you may not be able to do everything you'd hoped all at once—but you can do something.

If you're coming into the classroom with an orientation toward teaching for social justice, you already understand that public schools have historically often served as an oppressive force in the lives of poor children and students of color. I had that reality in mind when I started out as a new teacher, and I wanted to do my part to interrupt it. But my approach, at least initially, was naïve: If schools were oppressive, I figured, then the antidote to that was freedom, so in my classroom students would be "free." It sounded great in my head, but since I hadn't thought out the specifics of what freedom really meant within the context of a public school—or how I might create the conditions where it could happen—I quickly found myself in the midst of absolute chaos in my classes.

The problem with chaos is not only that it makes you crazy, but it directs all your energy toward anticipating and addressing student misbehavior. Other concerns, such as whether your kids are learning anything of value, tend to fall by the wayside. These skewed priorities are often reinforced by administrators who place a premium on order and control, and who hold up as exemplary those teachers who keep the tightest reins on their students. If you're not careful, you can find yourself falling into a similar pattern of thinking: classifying your days as good or bad based solely by how quietly your students sit at their desks or how straight they line up in the hallways.

Many young teachers are confident they'll be able to rise above such pressure once they have a classroom of their own, or delude themselves with the belief that they'll be viewed as such cool teachers that they won't have to worry about disciplinary issues. Progressive approaches to teaching often encourage such an attitude by glossing over classroom management concerns, or by suggesting that if teachers simply come up with engaging lessons, management issues will largely take care of themselves. But my experience is that, in many urban classrooms, it's far more complicated than that, and if you're blindsided by serious discipline concerns, as I was, it can be tempting to adopt draconian corrective measures. The point is not to obsess over order and control as a beginning teacher, but to go in with a specific plan of action for building community among your students rather than vague notions about "freedom." If you really want to have a collaborative and democratic environment in your classroom, you have to be thoughtful and purposeful in creating structures that support it.

These details of practice—creating an environment for learning, rethinking your curriculum, and fostering a democratic community—can all provide opportunities for bringing a social justice perspective into your classroom. But it's also possible to become lost in the everyday details, to get so caught up in the immediacy of your teaching that you don't pay enough attention to its larger contexts. Indeed, the undertow may pull you in such a direction: Professional development seminars and in-service workshops frequently encourage tunnel vision in new teachers by focusing narrowly on specific methods, strategies, or one-size-fits-all approaches.

That's why it's important to remind yourself that methods and other practical matters mean little unless placed within larger social, economic, and political contexts. For beginning teachers in urban schools—especially for those who are coming in as "outsiders" to the communities where they're teaching—committing to continued efforts at self-education on issues of race, culture, and poverty is vital (and also something you're not likely to get at an in-service). Middle-class teachers who lack a personal understanding of poverty and the many ways it can impact children, families, and neighborhoods need to do all they can to increase their awareness. Likewise, White teachers need to work hard to learn about the cultural histories and current struggles of their students of color and, at the same time, to examine their own privilege.

Still, no matter what you do to buoy yourself as a new teacher, you're almost certain to have moments—probably more than a few of them—when you question the value and effectiveness of what you're doing. One of the most persistent early challenges for a socially conscious teacher—at least it was for me—is fighting the feeling that your work isn't making a difference, or at least not the sort of difference you'd imagined. When your goals are expansive and hopeful, when you believe that teaching is potentially a world-changing act, it can become discouraging to feel as if your efforts are falling far short of that vision. As one young teacher I know put it, "You feel like you should be seeing light bulbs going off in kids' heads every day, like they're suddenly seeing the world differently. But a lot of times, you think, 'This whole week—nothing! I'm not teaching for social justice!'"

At times like those, the undertow pulls in the direction of fatalism, despair, and emotional disengagement. It beckons you to stop trying so hard, to be more "realistic" about the kids you teach, to abandon your belief that public schools can be transformed in any meaningful or lasting way. Resisting that suffocating pull—and holding on to hope instead—requires a delicate balancing act: acknowledging the grim systemic realities and personal limitations you face as a teacher, but at the same time re-committing yourself to working toward something better. You have to forgive yourself for your failings, then turn around and try to use them to re-focus and re-energize your teaching the next day. You also have to allow yourself to appreciate the good moments that do take place in your classroom—no matter how small they may seem in the grand scheme of things. In doing so, keep in mind the words of poet and essayist Audre Lorde:[3] "Even the smallest victory is never to be taken for granted. Each victory must be applauded, because it is so easy not to battle at all, to just accept and call that acceptance inevitable." I think every new teacher should have that quote taped to her desk, her classroom door, her rear-view mirror, her alarm clock—any spot where she might need a little extra strength for the journey.

Becoming a teacher is a journey, after all—one in which you're always learning. One thing I learned while writing this piece is that there's actually no such thing as an undertow. The force of water that pulls you down the beach is, in fact, called a longshore current, and the one that pulls you out to sea is known as a rip current. Undertow, it turns out, is a colloquialism. Considering that my mother was born on a farm in Georgia and raised in rural Kentucky, it makes perfect sense that that's the term she's always used. Longshore currents and rip currents will probably always be "the undertow" to me.

I learned one more thing, too. If you ever find yourself caught in a real rip current, the best approach is not to try to swim directly against it. You'll exhaust yourself, and the current's force will end up pulling you out anyway. Instead, say those who are knowledgeable in the science of wave motion, you should avoid panicking, swim with the current for a little while, and eventually you'll be free.

The undertow of schools, in my experience, doesn't release teachers from its pull quite so easily. Still, burnout being what it is, there is something to be said for new teachers not trying to fight it at every turn. The best advice, I think, is to choose your battles early on, pace yourself, swim with the current when you have to, and never lose sight of that spot on the shore.

Chapter 2

All Together Now

Two dozen 18-year-olds from across Illinois sit circled inside a classroom on DePaul University's main campus, nestled among the pricey greystones and trendy taverns of Chicago's Lincoln Park neighborhood. All are fresh out of high school, plan to become teachers, and are here to participate in a six-week summer institute—part of a scholarship program—that immerses them in city schools in the mornings and educational coursework in the afternoons. This class is called Diversity, and I—White, male, middle-class, and heterosexual—am the facilitator. On the face of it, not exactly a recipe for success.

Around the room, I've posted sheets of paper on the walls, each with a different heading: Puerto Ricans, people with disabilities, women, Muslims, suburbanites, and a dozen others. Each paper is covered with multicolored Post-It notes on which my students have scribbled stereotypes they've heard, at some point in their lives, about the listed group.

I ask for volunteers, and three come forward. I explain that I want them to walk along the wall, one at a time, pull a note from each category they identify with, then read it aloud and attach it to themselves. It's an activity designed to show how indiscriminately stereotypes can be applied—one I stole from a corporate diversity trainer. As was the case during my nine years of teaching middle school, few of my lessons for this class are true originals. I come up with one or two really good new ideas each year, but everything else is adapted, recycled, or straight-up swiped.

I recognize, of course, that the categories on the wall have a certain falseness about them. Though it's true, for example, that I'm White, male, middle-class, and all the rest, there's also more to me than any one of those labels—or any combination of them—might suggest. Over the course of six weeks, I plan to delve into these complexities more deeply with my students. But we have to start somewhere, so today, we're labeling.

"My name is Sherelle. I'm African American, so I'm loud," the first volunteer says as she plucks a note and places it on her shirt. She continues down the line, pulling off stickies and reading them as she goes. "I'm poor, so I live off the government. I'm a female, so I'm a bad driver. And I'm from a small town, so I'm closed-minded."

The two others follow. "I'm Luis. I'm a male, so I'm a jerk. I'm an immigrant, so I steal jobs from Americans. I'm a city kid, so I'm dangerous. And I'm Mexican, so I drive around in cars with 15 people inside."

"My name is Jenny. I'm from the suburbs, so I'm spoiled. I'm White, so I'm a racist. And I'm Catholic, so I'm—" She does a double take. "Sexually repressed?" The others laugh as Jenny reluctantly slaps the Post-It on her chest.

After several more students walk the line, we spend half an hour talking about how it felt to write down the stereotypes, to hear them read, and to have them applied to each other. Some students share personal experiences of being unfairly labeled because of skin color, accent, or religious beliefs. The conversation then shifts to how such stereotypes might impact them as teachers.

"It's just sad to know that there's people out there who really think those things," Jenny says. Several of the White students—who make up about half the class—nod in agreement.

"What do you mean, 'out there'?" Sherelle shoots back. "There's people in here who really think those things." That's right, I say in my head. Sherelle and myself included.

"Well, I just think people are people and kids are kids," says Jenny. "I don't care what color my students are. I love children. They're all the same to me."

* * *

When I agreed to take on the Diversity course, I wasn't sure what I'd gotten myself into. I first witnessed racial intolerance at a young age— growing up in North Carolina during the early years of desegregation—so I'd long believed that educating about human differences and social inequalities should be an integral part of what schools do. And I'd taught 7th- and 8th-graders in Chicago for several years by then, so I'd also seen first-hand how issues of race, class, culture, and language impact children's lives, both inside and outside the classroom. But how to pass these under-standings on to future teachers was something I hadn't much considered.

Before I took over, the class was known as Multiculturalism, and the course catalog stated that it was designed to focus on "celebrating the var-ied ethnic composition" of students in urban schools. Despite this sunny description, racial tensions had boiled over in the class during the previous summer, resulting in hard feelings and deep divisions among some partici-pants. The situation was so tense that the program's director considered dropping the course from the next summer's schedule. When I offered to give it a shot, he relented.

Born in the 1970s out of the civil rights struggle, the multicultural education movement spent much of the 1980s being dogged by critics on both the right and the left. But the political correctness of the 1990s brought widespread acceptance and, with it, a predictable watering down of multiculturalism's more radical elements. By decade's end, the term had been adopted by so many textbook publishers, school districts, colleges of education, and professional-development consultants that it didn't mean much of anything. As with phrases like "children first" or "life-long learn-ing," it became ubiquitous, nonthreatening, and—ultimately—empty.

The events of September 11, 2001, changed all that, thrusting multicul-turalism back into the political crossfire. The terrorist attacks reinvigorated those on both sides of the divide, arousing supporters and detractors alike to re-stake their ground and refresh their arguments. "Those people who said we don't need multiculturalism, that it's too touchy-feely, a pox on them," Judith Rizzo, deputy chancellor for instruction in New York City's public schools, told a conference audience while discussing bias incidents shortly after the attacks. "I think they've learned their lesson. We have to do more to teach habits of tolerance, knowledge, and awareness of other cultures."[1]

But if opponents of multicultural education indeed had learned their lesson, they weren't letting on. If anything, they were circling the wagons. Lynne Cheney, wife of then–Vice President Dick Cheney, said in a speech to the Dallas Institute of Humanities and Culture that, rather than embrac-ing multiculturalism, schools should place a stronger emphasis on teaching American history.[2] And Chester Finn, president of the conservative Ford-ham Foundation, wrote that it was "worse than nonsense" to promote a re-newed commitment to multicultural education in the wake of the tragedy.[3]

In the weeks following the attacks on the World Trade Center and the Pentagon, I visited several elementary schools to observe new teachers, and I didn't see much evidence that Cheney and Finn need worry. What I saw instead were lots of flags. Big flags, little flags, quilted flags, painted flags. The frenzy was so intense that a friend who teaches in a predominantly Mexican American community—and who didn't display the U.S. flag in her classroom—got a letter of reprimand from a substitute who'd taken exception to her apparent lack of patriotic spirit. "Your students look to you for direction," the note concluded. "In the mist [sic] of a national crisis our schools must instill unity in our students." It was the first time I'd ever heard of a teacher being admonished by a sub, but I guess I shouldn't have been surprised. As countless politicians repeated in the months following 9/11, extraordinary times inspire extraordinary measures.

But it's easy to sneer at such blatant nationalism. What's harder—extraordinary times or not—is to actually do something different, to nurture a classroom experience that is engaging and meaningful to kids, and that doesn't sell out to mainstream blandness. During my years as a middle school teacher, I struggled with that constantly. My efforts to help my students think critically, to provoke them to examine the constraints and possibilities of their lives, were far too sporadic. I'd rock the boat one day, then bail water for the next three.

As a teacher-educator, I still spend a lot of time bailing, but I've discovered that one of my strengths is an ability to empathize with novice teachers—mostly because I've fallen on my face so regularly in my own classrooms. When I talk with my summer students about the kind of teaching I believe in—teaching with a critical edge, with a political consciousness, with cultural relevancy—I never tell them it's easy. I only tell them it's possible.

* * *

"OK, I want everybody to find a partner." As soon as the words leave my mouth, a few students are already dragging chairs across the carpeted floor. "But hold up," I add. "One condition: I need you to pair up with somebody who identifies racially the same way you do." The chair-draggers slam on the brakes.

At this point, it would be easier to say, "OK, White people pair up with Whites, Blacks with Blacks, Latinos with Latinos," and get on with it. But because we've been discussing the complexity of identity in general, and of racial identity in particular, I don't want to take the easy way out. So I repeat: "Find a partner who identifies racially the same way you do."

Silent confusion reigns for a couple of seconds. "Oh, you mean like Black people with Blacks and Whites with Whites?" someone asks. I grin and shrug my shoulders, then watch as the students begin to pair up. Some move confidently. Others uncomfortably survey the room. Though they've acknowledged in the past that they self-segregate at certain times—in the dorms, on weekends, during social events—being asked explicitly to do so has made some people self-conscious.

After they've settled on partners, I check to make sure everybody's ready: two Mexicans here, a Korean and a Filipino there, two African Americans next to them, and—this being a group of future teachers—pairs of young White women all over the place.

Part of what I try to do in the Diversity class is to wake up the 18-year-olds a bit, push them to consider ideas some of them may not have thought about before, and, in doing so, clarify their reasons for teaching. This is especially important for White students, many of whom—though certainly not all—come from comfortable suburban subdivisions or two-stoplight towns. While such places are saddled with unfair stereotypes of their own, the opportunities they provide for Whites to interact with people of other races or cultures are often minimal. Many White students enter the class with cheery attitudes and good intentions, but they're usually expecting the sort of rah-rah positiveness associated with superficial gestures toward multiculturalism. Sing a stanza of "We Are the World," and be done with it.

Jenny's comment during the stereotyping activity exemplifies such an attitude. When she said it didn't matter what color her students might be, that they all would be the same in her eyes, I wasn't surprised. I hear variations on that theme every summer, and I know there are other students in the program who agree with Jenny. They hear her words not as an expression of naiveté, but as the crystallization of why they want to teach in the first place: They love kids. All kids. That's not only the summation of their budding philosophies of education—it's the whole thing. Part of my job is to help them understand that, though there's certainly nothing wrong with loving children, teaching is about a lot more than just that.

This is not to say I tailor my lessons to White students. Teenagers of color sometimes come in with their own limited experiences, and whether the topic is race, religion, or sexual orientation, it soon becomes clear that bigotry knows no boundaries. But as a White person myself—one who has struggled to better comprehend both racism and the unearned privileges I've received because of it—I feel an added responsibility to help White students become more aware of their blind spots. In that sense, being a White, middle-class, straight, male instructor has its advantages (or, you might say, its privileges). I can ask students to confront racism without Whites being able to dismiss me as an angry African American or Latino. I can also have them wrestle with homophobia without straight kids thinking I'm doing so out of a personal agenda. In other words, it's harder for those who need to open their eyes to simply turn away.

I display a poster at the front of the room, then pass out a photocopy of it to each pair of students. It's a collage of notable African Americans—120 of them, to be exact. Pictured are historical leaders such as Marcus Garvey and Mary McLeod Bethune, athletes and entertainers like Jesse Owens and Billie Holiday, and writers like Phyllis Wheatley. But no one is identified by name; each photo is accompanied only by a number.

I tell the pairs they have 15 minutes to see how many people they can identify. Renee and Karen, two White students seated next to me, simultaneously blow out exasperated breaths. "Oh yeah," I add. "And these people don't count." I reel off a list of ten names—Michael Jordan, Rosa Parks, Martin Luther King, Oprah Winfrey, and Bill Cosby among them—that I think even someone who's been in perpetual hibernation should recognize. "Thanks," says Ryan, another White student. "You just disqualified everybody I knew."

The next quarter-hour is a study in contrasts. Most pairs of African Americans struggle to recall faces, whispering names to one another, reminding themselves of each person's claim to fame, and compiling long lists. With few exceptions, everybody else just stares at their papers, shaking their heads, jotting down an occasional name.

"I think I know her. I just can't remember who she is."

"This guy looks familiar, but . . . "

"This is embarrassing," says Ryan, who I note has incorrectly identified Maya Angelou as Aretha Franklin.

When time is up, I call on Jonathan and Rodney to give thumbnail sketches of a few of the 45 people they were able to identify. Sarah and Jalisha then do the same with some of the 30-odd names they wrote down.

The scores for most of the White, Latino, and Asian duos aren't so impressive: six names, nine, seven. And some Black students are disappointed at their own lack of knowledge. "That's a shame," Nicole says to a friend. "At least these other people have an excuse. I'm Black. I should know this stuff."

Of course, identifying famous faces isn't the same as having in-depth knowledge of the African American experience, and I reassure the class that I'm not advocating a names-and-dates approach to teaching history. The poster is intended to symbolize some of what's missing in the standard curriculum, and they seem to get the point.

"I can't believe how much I don't know," Ryan confides to me at the end of class. If that's the only lasting lesson he hangs onto after these six weeks, I think to myself, it will still have been time well spent.

* * *

I'm teaching two classes of Diversity back-to-back on this afternoon, and the first one, which just ended, blew up in my face. After watching a documentary video about California's Proposition 187, whose proponents in the mid-1990s sought to deny education and other public services to undocumented immigrants, things got ugly fast. "I don't want to sound harsh," said Lance, an African American from rural Illinois, "but there's a lot of black people in this country who are Americans who need help. If these people are coming here looking for a free ride, they need to look somewhere else. We have enough problems of our own."

Despite Lance's disclaimer, his words did sound harsh, especially to many Latinos in the room. And after two other black students echoed his feelings, the session degenerated into an awkward and sometimes confrontational back-and-forth. I tried to steer the conversation in a more productive direction but with little effect. Arguments didn't exactly divide along racial lines: Keisha and Gabrielle, two vocal African American females, openly challenged Lance's views, and most of the White and Asian kids just kept quiet. But the air was thick with tension and, without question, racially charged. Worst of all, I could tell that some students had simply shut down, that too much was being left unsaid.

While teaching the Diversity class, I'm always a little on edge because I know that when you mix controversial topics with passionate feelings and disparate experiences, there's the chance that a fuse might get lighted.

But I'd never before felt this uneasy. It was one of the few times that I was actually watching the clock, begging the 90 minutes to hurry up and end.

Now, as the next class saunters in, I'm wondering if I should even show the video again. Part of me realizes that conflict is inevitable in this type of course and that I shouldn't try to avoid it. Another part, worried that bad feelings from the last class will spill over into dorm rooms, doesn't want to risk making things worse. One of my many aims in Diversity is to help build solidarity among students of color, to provide opportunities for them to see common threads in their experiences. I certainly don't want to cause deeper divisions. But after weighing both options, I decide to go ahead with the video. It's a powerful work—one I think my students should see.

Directed and narrated by a Los Angeles teacher, *Fear and Learning at Hoover Elementary*[4] looks at the impact of California's anti-immigrant initiative on students, teachers, and community members at Hoover Street Elementary School. Although Proposition 187 was eventually shot down in the courts, the xenophobic fervor it stirred up took on a life of its own, and the film depicts the damaging effects on the children of undocumented workers. In one scene, a White librarian tells five Latino students that he's watched conditions in the area get progressively worse as more and more immigrants arrive. "It's my country," he tells the kids, "and I want to take care of it." One child, stung by the librarian's words, snaps back: "It's not yours. It's everybody's." I've seen the film many times, but it never fails to leave me feeling frustrated and sad and outraged all at once.

After the video ends, the room is silent for what seems like five minutes. No one says a word. As I flip the lights back on, I notice that some of the Latino students are wiping away tears. Omar, a Mexican American who's said little in class all summer, slips out the door and into the hall. I'm bracing myself for another heated confrontation.

As with the last class, it's black students who eventually get the discussion rolling, but instead of kicking things off with defensive comments, they ask questions: What's the process immigrants have to go through to become citizens? What's a green card? Is there anything like Proposition 187 in Illinois? It's a gesture that opens up dialogue rather than shutting it down, and the conversation that follows has an entirely different feel. Latino students share their personal knowledge of immigration law, and others listen and learn.

As the discussion continues, Omar returns to the classroom, his eyes red. A few minutes later, he tentatively raises his hand.

"I don't wanna talk about the law right now, or about how people get their papers," Omar tells the group. "I wanna talk about my family." As soon as he gets these words out, he is convulsed in tears, openly sobbing. Judy, a Korean American whose father also immigrated to the United States, takes Omar's hand and holds it. Tears begin falling from her eyes, too. "I just went out in the hall and cried for five minutes," Omar continues, his voice trembling, "because I can't understand how there can be that much hate. I don't understand how people can have so much hatred for defenseless people who don't know their rights."

Omar's words spur others to share personal accounts. Across the room, Nelly tells of her father's struggle to provide for their family. "He's a landscaper, and everybody sees that as a degrading job," she says, starting to cry. "They look down on him. But he's an honest, hard worker." She and Manny, both from Mexican immigrant families, hold each other and slowly rock back and forth.

"My father will come up to me when I'm watching TV or something," says Judy, still hanging on to Omar, "and he'll hold out his hands, and they're really rough, 'cause he had to do a lot of manual labor when he first came over here. And he'll tell me: 'Feel these hands. This is what I've sacrificed for you.'"

Then Carlton, an African American who grew up in a Chicago public-housing development, raises his hand. "I just want to say that I have a lot of respect for Omar, and for the rest of you whose families have had to struggle like that. And it's hard for me to believe that this country . . ." His voice breaks off, and his eyes, too, begin welling up. He gathers himself. "If being an American means having that kind of hatred against another group," he continues, "then I don't want to call myself an American. I just . . ." He chokes up and, unable to continue, waves his hand as if to tell the rest of us to carry on. At this point, my eyes aren't dry either.

Tears, I realize, do not necessarily equate with learning. A bunch of crying teenagers might make for a good reality TV show, but it doesn't automatically translate into a meaningful educational experience. This class is supposed to be about edification, after all, not therapy.

But as the period winds down, and the talk circles back to equity issues in schools, I sense that the students are making connections. Perhaps a purely academic discussion about immigration would have produced the same results, but I doubt it. Could the White and Black kids in the class really begin to understand the ramifications of anti-immigrant initiatives *without* hearing stories like Omar's, Nelly's, and Judy's?

The positive vibe that's emerged from this group has picked up my spirits, but in the back of my mind, I'm still recalling the meltdown in the earlier class. When it's time to go, I decide to walk over to the dorm to check on a few people. On the way, I hear someone say that Diversity is the first class she's ever taken in which she's learned as much from other students as from the teacher. I consider it a compliment.

* * *

"This class has been an eye-opening experience," Melissa begins. It's our final session of the summer, and we're back in our circle of chairs, listening as each student shares parting thoughts. "Even though I've always viewed everyone as the same, and never had any biases or anything, it was still good to hear about the prejudices other people have."

One of the wonderful, and maddening, things about teaching is that you never know in advance what impact your work will have—or if it will have any at all. Whether you're working with kindergartners or adults, 8th-graders or college students, you undertake what you do, as educator and activist William Ayers puts it, "with hope and purpose but without guarantees." I've learned from teaching Diversity over the years—and this is not such a mind-blowing revelation—that the class is experienced differently by different people. What students take away from it depends, in some measure, on what they bring to it.

"I feel guilty and ignorant to an extent," says Andre. "I used to get all wrapped up in thinking that African Americans were the only neglected people in this country. But now I see that Hispanics are going through similar things every day. I guess I learned that we all face issues. Nobody has an easy road."

Juana is next. "One thing I was shocked about at the beginning was that there were people here who had never really come in contact with Mexicans before," she says. "But it was exciting in a way, 'cause I wanted to share my culture with them. I wanted to let them know how beautiful it is and how beautiful we are as a people."

"I think I came in here thinking racism was dead," Carly admits. "But now I see it's just more silent and subtle. I guess I was one of the 'sugarcoaters' who just tried to cover up the problems and pretend they weren't there. But they are, you know? And now that we're gonna be the teachers, we have to do something to change that."

At a forum I attended on zero-tolerance policies in schools, an audience member objected to the notion that schools can be reformed in any meaningful way. Trying to change practices and policies is pointless, he said, because the public school system was created to subjugate and control the masses, not educate them. In his estimation, the only real solution, the only way to truly change things, is through revolution—a complete overthrow of the capitalist system. Anything less is mere window dressing.

If I could write off a guy like that as a wacked-out Marxist, my work as an educator would be far less complicated. But I can't. On many levels, I agree with him. I know that too much of what I do—both with middle school students and future teachers—is superficial. I've heard people say that, in classes like Diversity, teachers spend too much time on identity issues—looking at things from an individual, psychological perspective—and not enough on institutional oppression and structural barriers to equality. They may be right. But, as I said before, I have to start somewhere. If I hit students with White privilege and colonialism on Day One, a few might be ready, but those who aren't might permanently tune out. And once people stop listening, what can you teach them?

If students leave my Diversity classes feeling more committed to respecting differences among people, to listening to alternate views, to learning more about other cultures, I won't complain. The world isn't such a kind place sometimes, and I'm all for any effort that promotes greater understanding. It may sound corny, and educators at both ends of the political spectrum may scoff, but it'd be hard to deny that such empathy is needed.

It's not all that's needed, though, and that's where efforts that call themselves multicultural often come up short. According to the editors of *Rethinking Schools*, a quarterly journal that focuses on issues affecting urban classrooms, multicultural education should be about much more than nods to diversity and tolerance. "At its best," they write in an issue that looks back on the movement's history, "multiculturalism is an ongoing process of questioning, revising, and struggling to create greater equity in every nook and cranny of school life. . . . And it is part of a broader movement to create a more equitable society. It is a fight against racism and other forms of oppression. . . . It is a fight for economic and social justice."[5]

I have no illusions that I always achieve such lofty goals with my Diversity classes, but I know that's the kind of education I'm after. Call it multiculturalism, call it teaching for social justice, call it what you want—labels don't matter all that much.

What matters is helping aspiring teachers begin to see schools as arenas of struggle and to see themselves as people who can bring about change. What matters is helping them understand that there's no such thing as a neutral classroom, that teaching, by its very nature, is a political act. We're all teaching for and against something, whether we choose to acknowledge it or not. Though I doubt they'd ever admit it, those who rant and rave against multiculturalism understand that all too well.

Chapter 3

We Don't Need Another Hero

When watching mainstream movies about teachers in city schools, it's tempting to stop following the predictable storyline and start playing "Count the Stereotypes" instead. With *The Ron Clark Story*,[1] a 2006 film based on the experiences of a former Disney American Teacher Award winner, you don't have to wait long for your tally sheet to begin to fill.

- When Ron (played by a smirking Matthew Perry) leaves North Carolina to pursue a teaching position in New York City, his small-town mother's last words are, "People get killed in New York."
- After Ron arrives in New York, the clerk at his apartment building tells him he'll need a personal injury lawyer if he plans to teach in the city.
- As Ron takes resumes around to different schools, he walks past a graffiti-covered wall while a police siren blares in the background. How else would we know we're in New York?
- At the second school Ron visits, called "Inner Harlem Elementary School" ("Inner" Harlem apparently sounding tougher than plain old Harlem), a teacher is—literally—throwing a troublemaking student out of the school's doors. How do we know he's a troublemaker? He's wearing a doo-rag.
- When Ron visits his students' homes to meet their parents before his first day of teaching, a flirtatious mom asks, "So, Mr. Clark, are you married?" while her son steals money from her purse in the background. The kids may have no morals, but they sure are crafty!
- At another student's home (following a shot of Ron walking past another tagged-up wall while a siren and rap music blare in the background), Ron asks a mom if she's willing to work with him

to help her daughter. "I already got a job, mister," the woman says sourly. "And four kids, and a brother on parole."
- Outside the school before Ron's first day, a quick montage (with generic hip-hop playing underneath) shows a barbed-wire fence, kids gambling, two boys fistfighting, and students bullying the only student who's reading—an Indian immigrant girl.

And all that just in the film's first 15 minutes. A little while later in the story, Ron arrives at his classroom one morning to find it ransacked, with messages from his students spray-painted (in multiple neon colors) on the walls: "Fool." "Go home teacher." "U suck." It's a scene that so strains plausibility that you'd think the producers would have left it on the cutting-room floor. His 5th-graders did this? How did they get into the school, not to mention the classroom, at night? And where'd they get all that paint? But apparently the filmmakers found it easy enough to justify: They're city kids. They're street smart.

The Ron Clark Story is far from alone in its transgressions, of course. Its exaggerated, stereotypical representations of city teachers, students, and families follow the formula of a long line of teacher-hero movies, from *Blackboard Jungle* and *Lean On Me* to *Dangerous Minds* and *Freedom Writers*. Thankfully, though, a few recent films centered on urban schools have charted a different course, and tell stories about city teaching that, in many respects, get it right.

＊ ＊ ＊

From the opening frames, it's evident that *Half Nelson*[2] isn't going to be a conventional "urban teacher" film. It begins on the hardwood floor of a bare apartment, where Dan Dunne sits in his underwear, legs outstretched, a scraggly beard creeping down his neck, a dazed, spacey look in his eyes. An alarm clock buzzes insistently in the background. It's time for Dan to leave for school, but he's struggling to peel himself off his living room floor. Soon, we understand why: In addition to being a social studies teacher and the girls' basketball coach at a Brooklyn junior high school, he's a crack addict, a basehead.

Dan wants to be a good teacher, and even when he's coming unglued personally—which is often—he does his best to hold it together for his students. In his classroom he ditches the prescribed curriculum and asks his Black and Latino kids to wrestle with tough questions. His methods are unimaginative—one part Socratic seminar, two parts didactic ramble— but his lessons push students to think, to make connections, to see history as something that can be shaped by everyday people working together and taking action.

Yet we're never tempted to see Dan as the savior, the White hero—and not just because of his drug habit. While it's clear that he despises the forces that keep his students down ("the machine," he calls it), the filmmakers remind us that he's not an innocent. When he asks his kids during class one day to name the obstacles to their freedom, their answers come easily: "Prisons." "White [people]." "The school." Then Stacy chimes in from the back row: "Aren't you part of the machine then? You White. You part of the school."

As committed as Dan tries to be to his students, it's obvious that he's holding on by a thread. He succumbs to his addictions at night and is distracted and tired in class the next day. It seems inevitable that his two lives will collide, and one evening following a girls' basketball game, they do. One of his students, Drey, a player on the team, finds him cowering in a bathroom stall, soaked in sweat, crack pipe in hand. She glares at him; he looks terrified.

"Can you help me up?" Dan finally mutters.

Drey gets him to his feet, then wipes his forehead with a wet paper towel. For a moment, we forget who's the teacher and who's the student. If anybody needs saving here, it's Dan.

But no miracle turnarounds or stand-and-cheer moments are to come. *Half Nelson* is too smart for that—subtle, understated, every note played in a minor key. It's a quiet film that takes the trite conventions of Hollywood teacher-hero movies and turns them inside out, revealing troubling contradictions and real-life shades of gray. Dan Dunne is bright, sensitive, politically aware, and has a genuine rapport with his students. He's also immature, unfocused, impulsive, and self-absorbed. Is he a good teacher? In some ways, yes; in others, probably not. That alone makes him far more believable than the saint-like, sacrificial protagonists of most urban teacher films.

Even in its smallest details, *Half Nelson* seeks complexity and plays against popular stereotypes. As Dan arrives at school one morning and gets out of his car, we don't hear sirens, gunshots, or a thumping hip-hop soundtrack. Instead, we hear the chirp of a lone songbird. Who knew the city had any? Later in the film, when Drey rides her bike past a row of desolate lots in her neighborhood, the overwhelming feeling is not one of menace or impending danger but of utter isolation and abandonment. It's the crippling aftermath of deindustrialization: factories shuttered, opportunities vanished, work disappeared.

What's freshest about *Half Nelson*, though, is its depiction of the reciprocal nature of the teacher-student relationship. Dan teaches and is taught, guides and is guided, receives as much as he gives. His students have much to learn from him, and they do—lessons about the clash of opposing social forces, about historical turning points and how change happens—but he, too, is a continual learner. Drey and the other kids help make Dan a better person than he would be without them. And in watching him, we learn that good teaching is not only about changing the world or changing the lives of others—it's about changing ourselves, a transformation from within.

For city teachers, it's also about functioning within—and challenging—a system that in many ways works to undercut and even thwart your best efforts. While the tyranny of high-stakes testing has made life difficult for teachers from the tiniest towns to the toniest suburbs, teachers in big-city schools often face additional hurdles and hardships. They must navigate added layers of administrative nonsense, do more with fewer resources, create community in overcrowded buildings where alienation and anonymity are accepted elements of school life. Teachers in city schools are far more likely than their counterparts elsewhere to have fewer desks than students, to have no planning periods (or even bathroom breaks) during an entire school day, to lack daily access to a school counselor or photocopier, or to be handed a scripted curriculum and told how and when it must be taught. To teach in a big-city school system is to recognize, as former New York City Teacher of the Year John Taylor Gatto[3] once said, that the institution itself has no conscience. And it is to understand, as Dan tells his students after showing them clips of 1960s Free Speech Movement leader Mario Salvo, that you sometimes have to throw your body on the gears of the machine.

* * *

But not all urban teachers recognize the churning of the gears or, even if they do, know what to do about it. *The Class*,[4] a French production that won the top prize at the 2009 Cannes Film Festival, serves as a particularly powerful example of this reality. The film drops us down inside the multicultural, multilingual, post-colonial mix of a middle school in Paris. Mr. Marin, the language arts teacher we follow over the course of a year, looks out on a group of students that in some ways resembles any middle school class you've ever seen: kids teasing, preening, sometimes openly defying—and then, out of the blue, making incisive comments that show how amazingly bright and perceptive they are. But this classroom looks different than Parisian classrooms of the past. It has students who are French-born, of course, but also immigrant kids from China, from the Caribbean, and from former French colonies and protectorates such as Mali and Morocco. Children at the crossroads in many, many ways.

Like Dan Dunne—though in very different ways—Mr. Marin is a bundle of contradictions. He allows plenty of student discussion in his classroom, but when push comes to shove (and it does), he still views himself as the sole dispenser of knowledge. One moment he's demanding that his kids be respectful and not use inappropriate language; the next he's dispensing biting sarcasm and put-downs to silence outspoken members of the class. Part of him seems well-intentioned in his efforts. Another part seems to view his teenage students as hopelessly uneducated and uncouth.

As far as his subject matter goes, Mr. Marin knows his stuff: He can effortlessly conjugate the imperfect indicative and analyze pieces of classic literature. But his approach to teaching—other than a couple projects that tap into students' outside-school experiences—is strictly traditional: teacher-directed, information-giving, vessel-filling. And for the most part it falls flat. When students question the value of the formal grammar structures Mr. Marin is intent on hammering into them ("Nobody talks that way," one says.), he gets defensive rather than trying to understand or entertain their critique. Time and again, he appears to have little idea of how to communicate the relevance of what he's teaching to the kids who walk through his classroom door each day. The teacher and his students may live in the same city, but they inhabit different worlds.

During one class discussion, Boubacar, a Malian immigrant, tries to explain to Mr. Marin why he isn't comfortable eating in front of the mother of one of his Muslim friends. The cultural and religious divide is stark, and Mr. Marin either doesn't know how to begin to bridge it, or doesn't think it's worth the effort.

"You can't understand," Boubacar tells him.

"I'm not smart enough?" Mr. Marin asks.

"No, it's not that," Boubacar says. "You just can't understand."

Indeed, these words encapsulate what many of the students in *The Class* seem to feel about the middle-class adults who manage and regulate their school days: You can't understand me.

The cultural and socioeconomic disconnect between teacher and students is nothing new in movies about urban schools. It's one of the hallmarks of the genre. But in lesser films, the challenge is usually conquered fairly quickly, with a gimmick or a memorable lesson that gives the teacher near-instant credibility. In *Dangerous Minds,*[5] high school English teacher LouAnn Johnson closes the cultural chasm with her Los Angeles high school students with an in-class martial arts demonstration. A few quick karate moves from the ex-Marine and the students realize, "Hey, this White lady may be cool after all." They begin to open up, and before you know it they're merrily dissecting Dylan Thomas poems.

One of the many things that makes *The Class* different is the nuanced way it deals with this teacher-student divide. Despite his intermittent best efforts, we never really see Mr. Marin turn a corner with his students. It's one step forward, two steps back. Moments of connection do happen: When Carl, a Caribbean immigrant who's had a troubled history at a neighboring school, transfers into Marin's class, the teacher disregards the hearsay about his new student. "We'll start from scratch," he tells Carl. Later, a memoir project Marin initiates energizes the class, and even briefly engages one of the most disaffected kids, Souleymane. But Marin never builds on this success. He doesn't "save" Souleymane—which would be the outcome in most Hollywood versions of this story. Instead, a violent in-class incident, precipitated in part by Marin's poor judgment, ends up sending Souleymane to an expulsion hearing.

More than any other fictional film I've seen, *The Class* captures the rhythms and the small moments—some funny, some uncomfortable, some heartbreaking—that make up a class period, a school day, a school year. Perhaps the most painful of these comes at the end, on the last day of school. Mr. Marin asks his students to share what they learned during the year and, one by one, they do. One talks about the convergence and divergence of the earth's plates, another about the Pythagorean theorum, a third about the triangular trade. Esmeralda, a wise-cracking student who's been a thorn in Marin's side all year, surprises him by telling him she's been reading Plato's *Republic* on her own.

When the final bell rings and the students leave, one girl, Henriette, stays behind. She's a quiet kid, one we haven't paid much attention to during the course of the film. "Sir," she tells Mr. Marin, "I learned nothing." Marin looks briefly stunned, then tries to reassure her. Of course you learned things, he tells her. But Henriette is insistent. "I don't understand what we do. None of it," she tells her teacher. The fear and confusion in her face speak volumes. She has been failed not just by Marin, and not just these nine months, but by a system that has allowed her to slip under its radar for years.

* * *

In the documentary film *The First Year*[6] (directed in 2001, somewhat ironically it now seems, by *Waiting for Superman*'s Davis Guggenheim), novice teacher Maurice Rabb gets a crash course in how the needs of a child can be crushed by the entrenched bureaucratic machinations of a mammoth school system. "I feel the pain of my students," says Maurice, who is Black, of his five-year-olds in South Central Los Angeles. As we watch his futile efforts to obtain help for Tyquan, a student with a severe speech impediment, we feel it, too. Maurice agitates to get Tyquan assessed by the school's frequently absent speech therapist, but months pass with no results. While his principal is sympathetic to his plight, she claims her hands are tied. The bigger picture, she says, is that the district is short 40 speech therapists, so their school is lucky to have one at all. Maurice makes phone calls to public clinics to try to get services for Tyquan, but there, too, he runs into a wall: the child's government insurance will cover only two hours of therapy per month. Frustrated and angry, but undeterred, Maurice begins one-on-one tutoring sessions with Tyquan three days a week after school. Progress is slow but certain. It's not enough, to be sure. But it's something.

Maurice's story demonstrates that resistance to schooling-as-usual doesn't have to take the form of grand or symbolic gestures. It can also be found in steady, purposeful efforts to make the curriculum more meaningful, the classroom community more affirming, the school more attuned to issues of equity and justice. Sometimes it means starting small: visiting the home of a troubled child, ignoring a senseless mandate, improvising to create a lesson that connects to students' lives. Other times it means joining with like-minded educators to form a study group, advocate for a policy change, or speak out at a board meeting. Either way, committed urban teachers learn that while they can't always tear down the wall that stands between their students and a truly humanizing education, they can chip away at it brick by brick.

Of course, not all city teachers face identical challenges because not all city schools are the same. In Chicago, magnet schools and college prep academies are inundated with resumes from qualified teachers and lavished with attention from community partners and politicians. Many schools in poor neighborhoods, meanwhile, struggle to stay alive amid threats of "takeover," and strain to attract the attention of outside partners or prospective teachers. A few elite Chicago public schools boast state-of-the-art facilities and technology; many others have sparsely stocked libraries, lack a functional science lab, and have no recreational space for students. These differences don't mean the selective and elite schools aren't really "urban." But they're a reminder that vast differences and inequities exist even within big-city systems, and for teachers in the most forgotten and forsaken schools, the journey toward equitable outcomes for children is an even steeper, more precarious climb.

Even so, urban teaching is not all toil and struggle—not by a long shot. For those teachers who remain in city schools long enough to get their bearings, the instances of utter frustration are tempered—and on the best days eclipsed—by moments of joy and transcendence. The obstacles are no doubt formidable for city teachers but, to borrow from James Baldwin,[7] the work is more various and more beautiful than anything anyone has ever said about it. How refreshing to finally see a few films that, in ways both various and beautiful, seem to understand.

Chapter 4

From the Trading Floor to the Classroom

Charlie's Story

It's a crisp October morning, and the sidewalk leading to Cameron Elementary School, tucked away on a residential street in Chicago's Humboldt Park neighborhood, is nearly hidden beneath a plush carpet of multicolored leaves. Inside the 1,200-student building, cast-iron radiators, their armor thickened over the years by countless coats of paint, hiss furiously as a class of 1st-graders ambles down the wide hallway's hardwood floors. On the west wall, a 12-foot piece of butcher paper proclaims in large letters, "Cameron students say no to guns," with the printed and sometimes scrawled names of dozens of children underneath. A girl with beaded braids near the back of the passing line pauses, smiles at me, and points to the banner. "My name's right there!" she says.

Up two flights of stairs, in Charlie Bright's 3rd-grade classroom, the sound of 25 pairs of scissors gnawing their way through paper fills the air. As students busily cut out alphabet tiles for a "making words" game, the 33-year-old African American teacher, dressed in a blue button-down shirt and pleated khakis, bounces from group to group to check on progress or hurry stragglers. Around the room, bulletin boards and displays of student work provide a glimpse into what the class has been up to: Venn diagrams comparing modes of transportation; drawings of the life cycle of a butterfly; a chart on presidential politics; and colorful campaign buttons for an upcoming class election. One student's button features a red background with blue balloons around the edges and the slogan "If you want to be free, just vote for Malik."

A couple years earlier, Charlie had been one of 18 "interns" in GATE (Golden Apple Teacher Education), an alternative-certification program I codirected for three years after leaving the classroom to work on my Ph.D.

A partnership between the nonprofit Golden Apple Foundation and the University of Illinois at Chicago (UIC), GATE provided an accelerated path for career-changing professionals to become teachers in Chicago schools.

When we began GATE, I had some reservations. I knew that some teacher educators were critical of the compressed timeline of alternative preparation programs, saying it was inadequate to prepare successful teachers—especially for city schools. "Would you want to be operated on by a surgeon who only had two months' training?" was a familiar line. It was a hard point to argue, but for me it was mitigated somewhat by the fact that our GATE interns would be supported via regular classroom visits and seminars throughout their first year, which few traditional programs offered. Besides, the opportunity to co-create a social justice–focused teacher preparation program, unencumbered by the usual bureaucratic constraints of undergraduate tracks, seemed too good to pass up. So, working with another doctoral student and our faculty adviser at UIC, I helped to develop curriculum, lead seminar sessions, schedule guest presenters and workshops, and provide interns with regular feedback on their teaching.

Charlie's GATE cohort was made up of people whose academic backgrounds, talents, and interests had taken them down a variety of paths: a cop, a filmmaker, an accountant, an army veteran, a nurse, a WNBA player, a media buyer/improv comic. Most had found success, or at least the promise of it, but for various reasons had decided to leave those occupations to pursue a teaching career. Charlie, who'd grown up in Chicago and graduated from the University of Notre Dame with a degree in sociology, had spent three years as a community organizer and three more as an options trader before deciding to make the switch. "I always knew I wanted to teach," he says. "I just didn't know how to get into it. I was already working, I had bills, I had a family—I couldn't afford to go back to school for three years."

Today, as Charlie's students get a bit too boisterous during the "making words" activity, cheering loudly each time they correctly spell a word with their letter tiles, he's quick to redirect their energy. "Remember, if you get it right, that's great," he says. "But instead of cheering, let's do this." He pumps his open palms toward the ceiling in a tame rendition of the "raise the roof" gesture. A few minutes later, after several students respond to Charlie's clue—"This word begins with a 'd' and means 'when something awful happens' "—by spelling "disaster," the roof of Room 304 is enthusiastically, if quietly, raised by a dozen pairs of brown hands.

Like all our interns, Charlie had his share of struggles during his initial year. He wondered at times whether the GATE approach, centered around the notion of teaching for social justice, was providing him with enough of what he considered practical preparation. Even in year three, he says, he still faces plenty of day-to-day challenges. "The difference is that when something would go wrong the first year, I would panic and I wouldn't know how to recover," he tells me. "Now I can think a lot faster."

Of course, moments of first-year panic strike traditionally prepared teachers, too. But Charlie's points are well taken. When we began GATE at UIC, my main concern was how best to prepare our interns to teach in city schools. My experiences in Chicago classrooms taught me that those actions considered the core of a teacher's work—explaining concepts, planning lessons, managing student behavior—are only small parts of a bigger picture. So while technical matters had to be addressed, we emphasized a social justice component to dedicate ample time to other, equally important, challenges. Among them were making room in the curriculum for students' voices and cultural backgrounds, building strong relationships with kids and their parents, better understanding the impact of poverty, and getting to know communities from an asset-based perspective.

As self-satisfyingly progressive as all this may sound, it didn't always go over well with our interns. Once inside classrooms, some thought that the "big picture" questions seemed unimportant when compared with more pressing concerns: How do you get a class of 2nd-graders to the washroom and back in less than 15 minutes? How do you help a kid who somehow made it to 5th grade without being able to read even a picture book?

Phylis McGarr, who worked as a nurse for 22 years before becoming a GATE intern, says she was expecting more of a "nuts and bolts" approach during the eight-week preparation phase. "During that first summer, I didn't feel like I was getting the 'This is how you do it' part," the 50-year-old recalls. "I looked at it like Maslow's hierarchy of needs—you have to learn the basics before you can build on them. So while you were talking about social justice, I'm thinking, But how do I teach?"

With two-and-a-half years under her belt as a teacher on her native South Side, Phylis says her rookie year was filled with doubts about whether her 2nd-graders were benefiting educationally. "There were many times when I would think, 'Oh my God, these poor kids. I'm not teaching them how to read.' And then one day, I just looked up, and they were all silently reading—even the kids who struggled with it." A smile crosses her face. "There was a calmness about them and an interest in reading. For me, it was a great moment."

Phylis says she's come to accept the notion that teaching is learned over time, in real situations with specific children. "I kept thinking it should be formulaic," she says. "But I realize now that it's not like that. I guess I look at it as research and development. You get a little more research behind you in the classroom and you can develop more programming that's appropriate—agewise and interestwise— for the kids."

* * *

I remember hearing Charlie Bright describe his first day as a teacher as being painfully awkward. "The kids were new to 3rd grade. I was new to *any* grade," he said. "It was kind of like being on a first date."

From the beginning, Charlie was a thoughtful student of teaching— observant, not afraid to reconsider his assumptions, never satisfied with his halting efforts to improve. He chastised himself when he resorted to busying kids with worksheets, wondered aloud at times about the depth of his commitment, and was forever his own worst critic. "I wouldn't want my own daughter to be a student in my class," he once said.

Now, as he flips on an overhead projector to begin an after-lunch math lesson, much of that self-doubt seems to have peeled away. He crosses the room, grabs a plastic shopping bag off the floor, and pulls out two new boxes of pencils. "We were running out of pencils again, so I went out and bought some last night," he tells the class. Tyler and Navarre, two African American boys sitting next to me, are all ears—as are the other kids. "Each box has six packs of pencils," Charlie continues, holding up one box for all to see, "and each pack has 12 pencils in it." Peering through wire-frame glasses, he writes what he's just said on the overhead as a word problem. "All right, let's see if we can figure this out," he says. "How many pencils are in each box?"

As Tyler and Navarre begin scribbling computations, I ask Tyler what he thinks of Charlie. "He a good teacher," says the 9-year-old, his long cornrows beaded at the tips. "He make us work hard. He be teachin' us 4th-grade stuff so when we get there, we gonna already know it." Tyler looks at the numbers he's written in his notebook, then adds: "And he don't never yell at people or throw us out the class."

At Cameron, where the student body is 44% African American, 54% Latino, and 97% low income, Charlie is the school's only black male classroom teacher. One of the original appeals of GATE, for me, was its potential to do what other alt-cert programs had proved was possible: attract a more diverse pool of candidates to the classroom. In Chicago, as in many other districts nationwide, people of color continue to be underrepresented in the ranks of elementary and secondary teachers, and the paucity of men on elementary staffs is well-documented. In our three GATE cohorts at UIC, 32% of the interns who completed the program and became teachers were African American, and 34% were male—far higher proportions than in UIC's undergraduate elementary certification pipeline during those years.

Charlie, who has 11 African American boys among the 26 students in his class, believes his presence at Cameron is important. "Most of my students are black, and I think they relate to me differently than they do to the White teachers," he explains. "And the black parents, I think they see that I'm not so quick to judge them. I think a lot of times they feel like they're being judged by teachers—and from what I've heard come out of the mouths of some of the teachers here, they are being judged sometimes. I think there are some teachers here who could definitely use some work on race relations themselves."

When it comes to the lives of his Mexican and Puerto Rican students, Charlie has had to put in extra work of his own. He says it's an ongoing process, but he believes he's been able to develop strong bonds with many Latino children and their parents. "One thing I took away from GATE is how important it is to know your students, to understand where they're coming from," he tells me. "I'm still struggling to do a better job of that. . . . When I meet with parents, I always say, 'I don't know as much about your child as you do—what can you tell me?' And I always learn something I didn't know."

After giving his students several minutes to deliberate on the pencils problem, Charlie returns to the overhead projector and asks for volunteers. The kids describe varying strategies: Some counted tally marks; others added six 12s together; one multiplied 12 and 6. "Good job, everybody," Charlie says. "All of those strategies can work. There's more than one way to do it."

That maxim doesn't hold, however, when it comes to assessing good teaching in Chicago. "What I've learned in the past two years is that most of the things that were valued in GATE aren't important to the people who evaluate me," Charlie says. "They want to know about test scores. They want to see core subjects. They want to see student writing on the wall, and they couldn't care less what the writing's about—as long as it's writing. I don't think I've been asked one time how I'm dealing with race in the classroom or how I'm building community. I know those things are important, but when I'm getting evaluated, that's the last thing they're looking for."

So how does he renew himself in such a narrowly focused environment? The kids, he says, "bring so much energy; they're so creative, and it's great to see when things are clicking, when a student who's been struggling starts to build himself up. . . . Given the right opportunities, I feel like these kids can do as well as anyone."

✳ ✳ ✳

Looking back on his GATE experience, Charlie gives the program high marks. He says he learned a great deal that first summer from his mentor teacher, and benefited from the regular observations and weekly seminars during his first year. Both of these, he says, gave him an edge over other new teachers.

But his reviews are mixed when it comes to the program's social justice curriculum. "I try to do the things we talked about," he says. "I try to teach from multiple perspectives, I try to use literature that relates to my students' experiences. But I still wish we would've done more with how to teach certain subjects, like math and reading. I definitely came in that first year feeling like I was missing some things."

Still, as I watch Charlie interact with students and listen to him talk about his work, I see and hear echoes of our GATE teachings. We chose not to make "nuts and bolts" our primary focus because of our belief that teaching is not a mechanical, by-the-numbers enterprise. As Martin Haberman, longtime professor of education at the University of Wisconsin-Milwaukee, has written, teachers in high-poverty schools fail not because they haven't learned how to conduct a direct instruction lesson; they fail, he insists, because they're unable to establish meaningful relationships with diverse groups of children.[1]

Charlie tells me that the most important thing he got from GATE was simple: the opportunity to teach. "I wouldn't be a teacher today if it wasn't for the GATE program," he says. "I'd still be managing trades at a discount brokerage house." While teaching is more difficult than he ever imagined, he says, he enjoys the challenge of coming up with new ways to engage his kids. "I think about it almost 24/7—what can I do better? How can I improve a certain lesson? Do I need to go to the library today? I'm constantly thinking about it. And every year, I'm getting better."

* * *

A week later, I'm back in Charlie's classroom during his morning literacy block. On the board, a chart informs students where they should be during each of three 20-minute rotations: two groups reading books of their choice, two more working on reading-response journals, and one in a guided-reading session with Charlie. He listens and takes notes in a three-ring binder as a girl who's practically buried beneath a hooded jacket makes her way through a passage, her index finger sliding across the page as she utters each word.

"Try to use just your eyes, not your fingers," Charlie gently suggests. "Trust your eyes. You'll read faster."

Almost everyone in the room is busy either reading or writing. Tyler is lying face down on a carpet, propped on one elbow, going through a response Charlie wrote to his latest journal entry. His feet, clad in Spiderman sneakers, kick back and forth in the air. Charlie's eyes scan the space every 30 seconds or so to make sure the groups are staying focused; occasionally he has to call someone out, but for the most part, the kids are absorbed in their work. "We're starting to get into a good rhythm," he'll tell me later.

I'm thrilled, of course, to see the kind of teacher Charlie is becoming, but I can't take credit for it. My contributions were a small part of a team effort during his time in GATE, and he's learned a great deal since then— from colleagues who've gone out of their way to help, from workshops he's attended, from his students, from experience itself. What GATE did, it seems to me, was open a door for Charlie and help guide him on the tentative first steps of his classroom journey—when many novice teachers are more or less on their own. He's taken it from there.

When I ask what he hopes his students will get from their time together, Charlie ponders the question before answering. "I hope that 15 years from now, when kids think about me, they'll say, 'In 3rd grade, I had a great teacher. He was fair, he respected me, and I learned lots of things.'" Charlie says that's how he remembers his own favorite teacher, whom he had in 7th grade at a Chicago public school. "I remember feeling like I was as well prepared as anybody that year," he continues. "I felt like I learned as much as any other 7th-grader in the entire city—or the entire country. And I hope my students can look back and say that, too."

Chapter 5

Seeing, Hearing, and Talking Race

Lessons for White Teachers from Teachers of Color

Starting out as a teacher, I knew I had a lot to learn. I'd come into the classroom after a few years working in video and television production, and I had no formal preparation in education. I hadn't thought much about how kids learn best or how to plan an engaging lesson. I didn't know any of the buzzwords. I had never even heard of John Dewey.

Yet even before one of my 6th-grade students growled at me to "Go back to North Carolina, White boy," I realized that my learning agenda as a new teacher had to include more than lesson planning, classroom management, and the other "practical" items one might imagine. As a White person and recent transplant from the South, I had just as much, if not more, to learn about the context of my teaching: the lived experiences of my students and their families, the social and economic landscape of the school's neighborhood, and the ways my work with urban kids would be impacted by issues of culture, language, class, and race.

Early on in my teaching, I was challenged and inspired by Paulo Freire's conception of a humanizing education that is co-creative in nature and "forged with, not for, the oppressed."[1] Emphasizing the importance of teaching as a dialogical process, Freire insists that genuine dialogue is impossible without humility on the part of all participants. "How can I dialogue," he writes, "if I always project ignorance onto others and never perceive my own? How can I dialogue if I consider myself as a case apart from others—mere 'its' in whom I cannot recognize other 'I's?"[2] Reading Freire reminded me that if I hoped to work in communion with poor families and people of color, I had to see myself as a continual learner, a teacher in the midst of an ongoing personal transformation.

I began to fill some of my gaps of knowledge by reading books and articles by Black educators who wrote specifically about teaching African American students: Janice Hale-Benson, Jawanza Kunjufu, and Lisa Delpit all helped me examine my teaching—and myself—in ways I hadn't before. I also learned a lot from entering into dialogue with Black and Latino colleagues who became my mentors and my friends. These were teachers who had inside understandings of the communities in which we taught, who saw the students in our classrooms not as "other people's children"[3] but as their own.

More than a decade later, I'm still working in Chicago schools—now mostly as a teacher educator—and I'm still listening and learning. I'm also trying to pass on some of what I've learned to pre-service and beginning teachers, many of whom, like me, are White and "middle-class," and find themselves in the unfamiliar role of "outsider" in the schools and communities in which they are teaching. Some recognize early on that they need to begin to rethink their biases and question assumptions they have long taken for granted. But they are often unsure where to begin. Other White teachers would rather avoid such topics altogether, and can be especially resistant to examining their own racial identity development and the ways racism plays out, both at the macro and micro levels, in city schools.

Jacqueline Jordan Irvine suggests that such avoidance is all too common among White teachers, many of whom, Irvine says, continue to cling to a "color-blind" approach in their thinking and classroom practice. Using this framework, teachers maintain that kids are kids, and that racial and cultural differences are best ignored so that all students can be treated in an "equal" manner. Issues of race, Irvine writes, are particularly difficult to confront for many White teachers, who are often "unable or unwilling to see, hear, or speak about instances of individual or institutional racism in their personal and professional lives."[4]

But according to four teachers of color in whose classrooms I spent time over the course of a school year, White educators ignore race at their peril. "Race is a big issue for [my] students," middle-school teacher Toni Billingsley told me one afternoon at her west side Chicago school, where the student population is nearly 100% Black. "And it affects their attitudes towards new teachers when they come in. I think the fact that I'm an African American female helps me relate to my African American students. I don't know if it's respect or what, but I think it makes it a little easier. I've seen some teachers who have had some wonderful lesson plans, who would be outstanding teachers, but one of the things that hurt them in the classroom was that they were White."

Billingsley went on to explain that the problem was not so much skin color as it was a clash of expectations: teachers who expected to be viewed as authority figures simply by virtue of their position, and students who believed adults should earn their authority by showing they knew how to exercise it. She was also quick to point out that a number of White teachers at her school had built strong, mutually respectful relationships with their students. Still, she was unequivocal about one thing: For teachers and kids in city schools—as in most any school in this country, really—race matters.

This continues to be an important dynamic to consider because, as has been well-documented, the teaching ranks of U.S. schools remain largely White even as the student population has become increasingly diverse racially and culturally.[5] Even in large urban systems, where teachers of color are present in greater numbers, their totals are still disproportionately low. In Chicago, for example, Whites comprise nearly half the city's teaching force even though 91% of the system's students are children of color.

So, what do White teachers need to learn, do, and commit themselves to in order to be effective with students who are racially and culturally different from themselves? The teachers of color I interviewed had a number of suggestions, but they would all agree that there is no simple set of rules to heed, no easy five- or ten-step plan. In fact, none of the lessons that follow are in any sense quick fixes for White teachers: It's not a matter of putting up a few posters that represent the cultural heritage of your students—though that couldn't hurt. Rather, the teachers I interviewed suggest changes to White teachers' belief systems, thought processes, self-concepts, interaction patterns, and classroom practices that are deeper and in many ways more personal, and thus require a greater commitment, a longer view.

Listen to Teachers of Color

The importance of listening to teachers of color may sound obvious, but the experiences of Black and Latino educators have shown otherwise. Lisa Delpit, in her discussion of what she calls "the silenced dialogue," quotes an African American teacher reflecting on her one-sided conversations with White colleagues:

> When you're talking to White people they still want it to be their way. You can try to talk to them and give them examples, but they're so headstrong, they think they know what's best for *everybody*, for *everybody's* children. They won't listen. . . .[6]

Cynthia Nambo, a Mexican American educator, told me she had confronted similar attitudes at workshops and conferences and at the schools in which she worked. On numerous occasions she had felt her contributions to pedagogical discussions being ignored or given token attention by White collaborators. Once, Nambo told me, she had taken a freelance consulting position with a nonprofit organization to assist in developing programming and curriculum for Latino teens. But it didn't take long before she began to feel shut down by the "compassionate superiority," as she called it, of her mostly White co-planners.

"Any organization has to look at the way they communicate," she said. "You have to go through a process of changing how you talk to people or else it's just a hierarchy. But these people weren't listening to me, and I was getting really frustrated. I'd come home and talk with my husband about it—because he's my sounding board—and he'd just be like, 'The whole world is like that so we just have to keep going.' And I'd tell him, 'Why am I going through this struggle with these people when they don't really want to see it?' You think the director of the project, who is a progressive woman and feels she is not racist, really wants to go through the process of me saying, 'You are being racist because you're not listening to me?'"

Even in the area of bilingual education—which Nambo not only studied extensively but to which she also has an intensely personal connection—she had seen her opinions disregarded by Whites who seemed to believe they had a clearer understanding of the needs of Spanish-speaking students. "I've been teaching for five years," Nambo said. "I was a counselor in my community for two years. I've done a lot of research, I've done a lot of study, I have a lot of experience in the community. Yet there are people who don't have the experience that I have and they are listened to. They don't even have the life experience that I have, and they're listened to. . . . And when I'm written off, it feels horrible."

As a White educator with experience in city schools, I have seen the flip side of the dynamic Nambo describes: I have been the person who *is* listened to, whose opinions and perspectives *are* valued. Though I try to be careful to explain that I don't view myself as an "expert" on multiculturalism or urban teaching, I am still sometimes introduced or perceived that way when I give talks or presentations to predominantly White or non-urban audiences. The combination of my experience teaching in the city and my social status as a White male seem to crown me as a specialist in the eyes of some, whereas the knowledge, expertise, and extensive life experiences of teachers such as Nambo are often not given the same credence or authority.

Nambo believes that White administrators and teachers who work with Latino children need to examine the ways they communicate, and work harder to ensure that they are listening to—and hearing— the voices and perspectives of Latino colleagues, parents, and community members. That means taking proactive steps to invite those voices into dialogue, and attending carefully to conversations among people of color that are already underway.

In either case, for White educators it means learning to listen more than you talk. It also means pushing yourself out of your comfort zone: *Why are all the White teachers sitting together in the faculty lounge?* is, in some schools, a question that needs to be asked. Delpit sums up the need for increased cross-cultural dialogue this way: "[A]ppropriate education for poor students and students of color can only be devised in consultation with adults who share their culture." She adds, "Good liberal intentions are not enough."[7]

Examine Privilege and "Whiteness"

Substantial privileges come with being a White person in America— unearned benefits that someone like me accrues simply by virtue of my skin color. It is a concept that many Whites find threatening because it calls into question the myth of the level playing field. While some White people are willing to acknowledge that people of color continue to be disadvantaged in a variety of social arenas, they are less inclined to concede the inverse: that they are inevitably advantaged as a result. Racial profiling by police or other law enforcement agencies, for example, not only harms African Americans, Latinos, and Arab Americans—it also *benefits* Whites who aren't targeted. This distinction, however, is often lost on the beneficiaries. Indeed, it has been said that privilege for Whites is like water for fish: It's all around them, but it's hard for them to notice it.

The refusal to acknowledge and confront privilege, says Mexican American middle school teacher Nancy Serrano, was common among the White students in her undergraduate education courses. "We'd be in class, and they'd be confronted with issues," she says, "and even then they'd *choose* to ignore them. I mean, there were always White people who were involved, who were active, but they were only a few. The majority were closed-minded, and they didn't want to open up. They had this utopian view of the world and they didn't want to shatter it. They chose to remain ignorant."

History teacher Liz Kirby, who is African American, has seen the same sort of willful ignorance play out in teachers' classrooms, and she says it can inhibit White teachers from effectively reaching Black students. "Some White teachers aren't really aware of their own privilege," she told me. "They haven't begun their own critical self-examination. To teach Black kids well, a White teacher has to be able to say, 'I know I'm White and this can get really complicated, so let's talk about why that could be.'"

When White teachers begin to examine their own racial identity in serious and sustained ways, writes Gary Howard, they can "come out of the closet of ignorance and denial" and begin to "gain credibility" with students and colleagues of color.[8] When they don't, the result can be teachers who, consciously or not, see the world exclusively through their own racial, cultural, and class-based lenses—a tendency that may lead them to interact with students and families in detrimental ways. A teacher friend once told me of a White colleague's advice to a Mexican immigrant student who was having trouble getting his homework completed: "Just go in your room, close the door, shut out all the noise, and focus on your work." That the student didn't have a room of his own or a door to close apparently never occurred to the teacher. More recently, another teacher I know listened as a White counselor expressed her dismay at what she perceived as the limited experiences of some of her school's Mexican American students. "I can't believe these kids haven't been to Navy Pier," the woman said, referring to a downtown Chicago tourist attraction. "Their parents don't take them places. When I was little, my mom would pack up the car and take us to Grant Park." She added, "And we weren't rich, either. But she still took us places."

Such responses grow out of an often subconscious worldview that takes for granted a White, middle-class, English-speaking frame of reference. Examining previously unrecognized social advantages and privileges can help White teachers question such notions and recognize, as anthropologist Wade Davis has said, that the "world in which we live does not exist in some absolute sense, but is just one model of reality."[9] Understanding the limitations of their own perspectives may in turn help them work with students of color and their families in more authentic and respectful ways. But like learning to teach, the process of confronting one's privilege and redefining one's Whiteness is a continual one.[10] For the committed White teacher—myself included—it's an ongoing project.

Be Honest About Gaps of Knowledge and Commit to Learning More

In addition to learning about themselves, White teachers in urban schools must commit themselves to becoming "students of their students"[11] and students of the communities in which they do their work. One way to do this is to make a conscious effort to become well versed in the histories and literary traditions of the cultural groups in your classroom. Another way is to make students' lives and experiences an explicit part of the curriculum. Liz Kirby told me that she begins each school year by trying to learn as much as she can about her teenage students. "My first weeks of teaching," she said, "are all about who my students are, where they're coming from, what they believe, what they're afraid of, what they want to learn, how they learn best—those kinds of things." But Kirby believes White teachers are sometimes afraid to delve into students' backgrounds in the classroom if they think such explorations might touch on matters of race. "I think there's a fear of how kids will react," she says. "Classrooms are such emotional spaces anyway, so I think people figure why bring in race when you feel like you'll never be able to talk about it in a way that's healthy or that solves anything. Why open up the can when you don't know what's going to happen with the worms?"

Still, Kirby believes that despite their uncertainty, White teachers must be willing to say to Black students, " 'I know I'm really ignorant about your experience, but I want to know, and I'm open to learning, even though some of what I learn may be hard for me to understand or painful for me to hear.' " Teachers who are honest about their own gaps of knowledge and who demonstrate a sincere desire to learn, Kirby says, will gain their students' respect. "Kids can read you," she says. "They can tell if you're really trying to understand or if you're just going through the motions."

Kirby's observations are echoed in an interview I did with a former student, Lourdes, about her experiences at a Chicago public high school.[12] While she expressed frustration over the lack of a critical perspective in the history classes she'd taken, Lourdes singled out a new English teacher who'd shown a keen interest in learning about her cultural background:

> She's just out of college—a Caucasian—and she's pretty cool. She makes us write journals. And one day she told us to write down three things from our culture and how we recognize them. So one of the things I wrote about was the music, about *mariachi* and all that. And after she read mine, she started asking me questions. She said she had seen a group like *mariachis*, except it was all guitars. And I explained to her that that was *rondalla*. And she was like, "Yeah, I like that." And she brought over a piece of paper and she made me write it down. 'Cause she really wanted to learn, you know?[13]

Angela Valenzuela, in her study of the damaging impact of what she calls "subtractive schooling" practices on U.S.-Mexican youth at a Houston high school, writes that "a community's interests are best served by those [educators] who possess an unwavering respect for the cultural integrity of a people and their history."[14] That requires a sincere and committed effort on the part of "outsider" teachers to put themselves in the role of learner. But it is far from impossible.

Clarify Purposes for Teaching

Many of the White pre-service teachers with whom I have worked initially cite a love of kids and a desire to help as their primary motivations. There is nothing wrong with either of those: in so many corners of the world—and in most of our own backyards—more love and more help would go a long way. But to work effectively in urban communities of color, teachers need not only a caring heart, but a critical eye as well.[15]

I've heard Nancy Serrano speak to groups of aspiring Chicago teachers on several occasions, and—especially if most of those in her audience are White—she challenges them to look critically at their reasons for choosing a life in the classroom. "You have to ask yourself why you're becoming a teacher," she says. "What's your purpose? Is it just because you think you love kids? Is it because you think you'll have short work days and summers off? Or is there more to it? You really have to ask yourself those questions."

Serrano's own purposes were framed by her experiences growing up poor on Chicago's South Side and the anger she felt when teachers and counselors at her public high school sold her short. "That's why I decided to become a teacher," she says. "I wanted to change things." In college, she was captivated by Paulo Freire's notion of an emancipatory pedagogy that aims to help students gain a critical consciousness. "I want [my students] to question, to understand themselves in this world, to understand why things are the way they are, and to be able to use that to overcome whatever they need to overcome," Serrano told me during her first year in the classroom. "I want them to understand the system so they can look at it and say, 'You know what? That's not right.' I want to let them know that a better future is possible."

What Serrano wants for her students, White teachers must desire to develop in themselves: a questioning mind, a critical consciousness, and a greater understanding of the systemic factors—disingenuous educational policy, unequal school funding, gentrification, complacent public officials—that impact communities of color and city schools. For those whose childhood experiences with public schooling were largely positive or at least benign, learning to see this bigger picture may not come easily. While Serrano's "political clarity"[16] was formed partly through exposure to critical perspectives in college, it also grew out of her personal experiences with discrimination and with public schools that—at least in some ways— failed her. Because middle-class White teachers typically have not had such life experiences, they need to make concerted efforts to expand their sociopolitical consciousness in other ways,[17] and to use that newfound awareness to sharpen and refine their purposes for teaching children of color.

Challenge Students—Don't Pity Them

A recurring refrain with all the teachers I interviewed was the high expectations each held for her students. "I push them—I mean, I *really push them*," Cynthia Nambo remarked of her 6th-graders. Toni Billingsley wasn't satisfied with simply giving her students "an experience" with Spanish—she wanted them to have the power that came with fully acquiring a second language. In Liz Kirby's room, the atmosphere of academic rigor was unmistakable from my first visit: "It's going to be an intense quarter," she told her students that day. "So please prepare yourself for that intensity." Nancy Serrano said she saw herself as an older sister to her students. "I don't let them get away with things," she told me. "I'm hard on them. Academically, I'm hard on them because of my own experience. I went to college unprepared."

It is important to remember, however, that, at least initially, kids may not appreciate being pushed beyond their accustomed limits. When Serrano asked her eighth-grade students to write evaluations of her language arts class during her first year, one boy scribbled a vehement protest. "I think this class is a piece of good for nothing class," he wrote. "I don't know why we have to do so much writing. People ain't going to look at how we write. DON'T THINK WE LIKE TO BE CHELLANGED!"

Serrano told me the letter made her question the tough demands she had placed on her students and scrutinize her motivations. "But most of all it just made me sad," she said. "Somehow this kid has been going through his education and getting by without being challenged, and he's gotten to the point where he's fine with it. . . . It's just sad to see that some kids are conditioned to expect less of themselves, and they get mad when somebody asks them to expect more." In the end, Serrano decided to relent only slightly: Instead of three or four pages of writing a night from her students, she agreed to settle for two.

The angry letter notwithstanding, these teachers' students typically did rise to meet the challenges set before them. In fact, one of the most profound realizations I had while observing in their classrooms was that while I thought I had set high standards for my Black and Latino students during my years as a Chicago teacher, I had not pushed nearly hard enough. Too often, I had let my students' tough circumstances reduce my expectations, consciously or not, to more "realistic" ones—an all-too-common response of well-meaning "progressive" teachers. Of course, being aware of students' outside-school challenges is essential. But feeling sorry for them and allowing them to *not* learn—granting them what Gloria Ladson-Billings calls "permission to fail"[18]—is something we must actively guard against. Teachers need to do all they can to understand the forces that constrain their students and show compassion for their situations, but at the same time they must arm students with the necessary tools to push against those constraints with all the force they can muster.

Be Resilient

As I mentioned at the outset, if there is one common thread that runs through all of the above "lessons," it is that none of them are changes a teacher can expect to make overnight. Each requires a deep and abiding long-term commitment. Indeed, when I asked Toni Billingsley what she thought distinguished the White teachers who found success at her school from the ones who didn't, her initial response was simple: They stay.

"[It's] because they hang in there," she explained. "From Day One, you can tell that they care about the students, and they stick in there. They're not going anywhere. See, with these other teachers, after a year, they left. And to the kids, it's like, 'Oh, you're another White person who's abandoning us. You're trying to save us, you think that it can't be done, and then you leave us. You're not willing to stick with us.' "

Buying into the myth of the White savior has sunk many novice urban teachers, even as it is perpetuated in popular films and books about teaching. But despite the familiar Hollywood storyline, children of color don't need to be rescued by anyone. They need opportunities and steady support—not heroics. While "saving" someone is often imagined as an act that happens swiftly and boldly, that is not how real teaching works. Teaching *alongside* urban students—learning from them and with them—is something that can only happen over time as trusting and mutually respectful relationships are built. So while there is much more to being an effective teacher than simple stick-to-it-iveness, the importance of Billingsley's notion of resilience should not be underestimated. Learning to teach is a commitment, and part of what makes good teachers better is the willingness to hang in there when the going gets tough.

The going can get incredibly tough for any new teacher, of course, no matter how she identifies herself racially or where she chooses to do her teaching. Teachers of color can wear their own blinders with regard to issues of class, gender, language, and even race, and it should be underscored that every educator, no matter what his or her cultural background, must stay awake to the ways social realities and inequities impact children's lives—both inside and outside school classrooms. No teacher should be exempt from the hard work of critically examining himself and the larger social contexts of his teaching. In that sense, the lessons related here may be useful, with certain caveats or modifications, for all teachers.

Even so, White teachers working in urban communities of color undoubtedly face unique challenges. But there is no prescription for success in such a scenario, and none of the teachers I have quoted here intended their suggestions as such. Moreover, they all understood that White teachers are no more a homogeneous collective than any other group, and to speak of them that way—as I have done here in certain respects—is an oversimplification. A pair of White teachers who begin their careers on the same day at the same urban school, for example, may be at quite different places in their racial identity development process and in their journeys as reflective educators.

Still, we have to start somewhere in thinking about cross-cultural teaching, and for many White teachers—again, myself included—listening to and learning from educators of color has proven to be a good place to begin. Doing so, as Lisa Delpit writes,

> takes a very special kind of listening, listening that requires not only open eyes and ears, but open hearts and minds. . . . [W]e must learn to be vulnerable enough to allow our world to turn upside down in order to allow the realities of others to edge themselves in to our consciousness.[19]

That alone will not transform schools into places where all children are seen as beautiful and valuable, where each student is viewed as being capable of deep understanding and challenging academic work. But if we listen carefully and act purposefully on what we hear, we'll be headed in a promising direction.

Chapter 6

Fire and Water

Reflections on Teaching in the City

I'm not sure I ever had the fire to teach. That's probably not the best way to begin, but don't misunderstand: I was passionate about my work. During my years teaching 7th- and 8th-graders on the South Side, I did my best to be a thoughtful, creative, and dedicated educator. But I didn't teach like my hair was on fire, as one currently popular book recommends. It's a catchy image, sure, but it's not an approach that will work for everybody, and it definitely wasn't my style. If you interviewed my former students, I doubt any of them would describe me as being "on fire" or "fired up" about my work. I think they'd say I was devoted to it, though, and that I cared deeply about their learning and their lives in my own, noncombustible way.

My wife would say that, as a person, I'm more water than fire, and she's probably right. Thinking back, many of the teaching metaphors that have resonated with me most strongly have been water-related. I remember during my early years in the classroom saying that I felt like I was drowning, or that I was trying to keep my head above water (one of my favorite songs at the time, which I always thought spoke to my work as a teacher, was De La Soul's "Tread Water"). As I gained more experience, I paid more attention to the "flow" of my classes and my day. And I often compared teaching in city schools to swimming in an ocean's undertow: trying to hold onto a student-centered vision of education when so much of the school environment dragged you in a different, more mechanized direction.

So, yeah, I'm more water than fire. But that doesn't mean I didn't wrestle with the question of how to keep on keeping on as a teacher. Rivers can run dry. Raindrops evaporate. Like most teachers I know, I had to find ways to stay invigorated in the classroom, to fight off feelings of frustration and despair, to come back ready for another try on Tuesday when I had spent Monday just trying to stay afloat.

One of the things that kept me energized during my first few years was holding on to the belief that, with a mixture of patience, perseverance, and hard work, I could somehow close the gap. No, not the achievement gap. Important as that is to keep in view, the gap I had an eye on at the time was a different one: the distance between the sort of classroom I envisioned in my mind and the one I actually stepped into each morning. It was, on many days, a yawning, gaping chasm.

In the classroom I dreamed of, the curriculum was co-created with my students, propelled by their questions and experiences but still connected to the "classical" knowledge they'd need to navigate the world beyond their neighborhood. The space hummed with activity, as small groups of kids collaborated on a variety of multilayered projects. Other students eagerly explored individualized topics of interest. Kids' voices were heard and valued, their minds were stretched and challenged, and each child felt affirmed as part of a supportive classroom community.

Then I woke up.

In my actual classroom full of real 13- and 14-year-olds, I too often failed to engage my students in anything that might shake them out of the predictable routine we called school. If my plans started to unravel, I sometimes resorted to using the same deadening techniques I'd seen other teachers employ: demanding silence (and usually not getting it), passing out mindless worksheets, lecturing the kids about how disappointed I was in them. Teaching, as I did, in buildings where "the pedagogy of poverty" was in widespread use, I too often found myself surrendering to a misguided quest for control, all the while losing sight of the larger purposes of my work.

Occasionally, though, I did catch glimpses of the classroom I'd imagined. During my first year, a group of my students orchestrated a mock trial, in which they charged the school with discriminatory practices: While teachers were allowed to bring drinks into the school's un-air-conditioned classrooms on hot days, students weren't. To make matters worse, a two-tiered menu existed in the lunchroom: one for students, and another, marginally tastier one for adults. Had it been up to me, I would have probably chosen what I thought was a more "important" issue for the trial—police brutality, say, or disinvestment in the local community—but to my students, the food-and-drink double standards were immediate and real injustices, and the intensity and spark they brought to the mock trial were genuine. It was one of the few times that first year I could point to something that transpired in my classroom and say, "That's how I think school should be."

I held onto moments like the trial as testaments to what was possible in my classroom. As years went by they happened more frequently, but never as often as they had in the classroom I dreamed of creating. It was a constant ebb and flow—good days and bad, ordinary lessons and inspired ones, kids engaged one moment and distracted the next. Still, keeping an eye on that imagined classroom, inching toward the kind of education I knew my students deserved, was part of what kept me going when things got toughest, even if I doubted I'd ever get there completely.

∗ ∗ ∗

At some point during my first few years as a teacher, my mother, who lives in North Carolina, mailed me a card to encourage me in my work. I don't recall if it was in response to a particular incident I'd told her about or if it was just one of those random kindnesses of hers, but whatever prompted it, I kept the card taped to my refrigerator for many years. On the front was a quote from Thomas Merton. It captured an idea I'd thought about a lot in relation to my teaching, but hadn't quite been able to put into words.

> Do not depend on the hope of results. When you are doing the sort of work you have taken on . . . you may have to face the fact that your work will be apparently worthless and even achieve no result at all, if not perhaps opposite to what you expect. As you get used to this idea, you start more and more to concentrate not on the results but on the value, the rightness, the truth of the work itself. . . . [G]radually you struggle less and less for an idea and more and more for specific people. . . . In the end, it is the reality of personal relationships that saves everything.[1]

In the current educational climate, of course, Merton's words sound hollow, if not naïve. Results, usually in the form of standardized test scores, are all that seem to matter these days. Personal relationships? Too touchy-feely in the era of corporate-style reform, No Child Left Behind, and Race to the Top. We're repeatedly reminded that our success or failure as teachers is all about results, test scores, the bottom line.

As much as I despise standardized tests, I wasn't unconcerned with them as a teacher. I understood, for example, that higher test scores were an entry ticket in many ways for the kids I taught, and I was happy (and, to be honest, often relieved) when my students' scores increased. But more than that, I wanted good things for my students beyond the narrow bandwidth measured by a single exam. I tried to help them develop tools for thinking more critically and making sound decisions in their lives, and I was thrilled when something turned out well for any one of them.

But results weren't what kept me going as a teacher. They couldn't have. Things often didn't play out the way I'd envisioned, and if I'd pinned my hopes to attaining only "superior" outcomes—especially as narrowly defined by test scores—I probably wouldn't have lasted long. Some might say that's caving in to low expectations, but I don't think so. I'd say it's acknowledging the reality that a single teacher can't change everything. Even when you do make a difference in a kid's life, you don't always know you've done so. Some things in teaching you just have to take on faith.

I'm reminded of a group of volunteers who run a turtle protection program in Holden Beach, a coastal town in North Carolina that my family sometimes visits. For hundreds of years, loggerhead turtles nested there without assistance, but because of pollution, poachers, and coastal development they've become an endangered species. So the volunteers, mostly retirees, have organized to help give the baby turtles a fighting chance. They build screens to protect the nests of eggs from raccoons and other scavengers. If eggs are laid in a spot that is susceptible to erosion, they carefully transport them to a safer location. And on nights when a nest "boils" and up to 120 hatchlings come squirming out, the volunteers are there, too, flashlights in hand. The turtles' instinct tells them to crawl toward the brightest horizon—the White foam of the breaking waves—but lights from beach houses can confuse them and send them off in the wrong direction. To make sure that doesn't happen, a volunteer stands ankle-deep in the ocean, shining a flashlight on the water as an extra guide. Other volunteers, as many as 15 or so, line a path to the surf, making sure the hatchlings don't get sidetracked.

I've watched this drama unfold, witnessed the tiny turtles scurrying down the sand toward the ocean, and while I'm sure the volunteers hope for the best for each of the newborns, the reality is that they never know the results of their patient, steady efforts. My guess is that, as Merton suggests, they focus instead on the value, the rightness of the work itself. As a teacher, I tried to do the same.

Of course, there's a big difference between teaching and protecting turtles. Like most metaphors, this one begins to break down if scrutinized too literally. The point, for me, is that a teacher's work must be at once grounded in the challenges of the present moment and directed toward the hope of a better future, of what might be. In that respect, the saving grace, always, is the kids themselves. As Merton expresses so eloquently, it's personal relationships, in the end, that make most everything worthwhile. To be sure, plenty of other important matters demanded my attention in the classroom: what to teach, how to teach it, how to create an affirming learning environment, how to keep an eye on the larger contexts of my work. But none of those meant much, I learned, unless they were informed by strong, mutually respectful relationships with my students.

That's not to say that my relationships with the kids I taught weren't sometimes maddening or contentious, or that my efforts to make connections with students were always successful. Robbie, a 7th-grader I taught toward the end of my time in the classroom, was being heavily recruited by the neighborhood gang, and in my reading class I saw him drifting slowly away. I tried to draw him back in, inviting him to stay after school to listen to CDs in my room, talking with his mom to get insight on what was happening at home, loaning him a book I thought he'd like, and taking him and a friend to browse at a nearby music store.

It seemed to be helping, until one morning before school a radio news broadcast I was only half listening to suddenly had me frozen: "Double murder last night . . . 14- and 15-year old are dead . . . teenager in custody . . . police say it could be gang related." The address the announcer gave for the crime wasn't far from my school, and when I heard it I felt my stomach tighten. I was worried that one of my students might have been killed. When I arrived at school a few minutes later, a colleague filled me in on the details. Indeed, two young men from the neighborhood had been shot dead. Robbie had been arrested for their murders.

That may seem like an unusual story to share. After all, wouldn't a tragic episode like that push someone away from teaching rather than keep them in it? You might think so, but if a big part of what's keeping you there are the relationships you've built, it doesn't work that way. Because even after a horrific, unimaginable event such as what happened with Robbie, life goes on for your students. So, later that morning in my third-floor classroom, I found myself sitting quietly with Robbie's classmates, feeling the weight of his empty chair, not knowing what to say, or how to make it better, but sensing that being together in the silence was, at that point, the most any of us could do.

The next week, one of my colleagues organized students to write cards and collect donations for the families and friends of the two teens who had been killed. The kids in my reading class, knowing Robbie's 13th birthday was approaching, made him a giant card, and a few wrote individual letters to let him know they were thinking about him. I dropped everything off to him at the juvenile detention center a few nights later. We didn't have much of a conversation, but again, it seemed like the important thing was being there. I remember him smiling when he read the card.

It wasn't one of those moments you see in movies about teachers—the ones that, even if you know better, make you want to stand up and cheer. But it's part of the ebb and flow of real life in classrooms. Joy and heartbreak, tedium and excitement, flashes of inspiration, and moments of darkest doubt—all carrying you along for parts of the teaching journey, pushing you onward and drawing you back again.

Part II

Youth on the Margins

Chapter 7

Juan at 16

Juan and a dozen teenage and adult students are gathered around the raised hood of a dilapidated Chrysler—the kind of beat-up vehicle the students I taught my first year would have referred to as a "hooptie." These guys call it a "beater," or a "rammer"—a ride that could be easily used for ramming others because, hey, what's one more dent? The car's body is scratched and battered, and its faded paint job indicates a distant past life as a taxicab.

It's the third week of a ten-week course on auto mechanics for beginners, a class that Juan, one of my former 8th-grade students, signed up for through the Chicago Park District. The class is being held at a park several miles southwest of his neighborhood, Back of the Yards, in a community of tightly packed brick bungalows on the western edge of the city. Outside the garage, a group of junior high girls are being led through a new cheerleading routine. In the main fieldhouse, a co-ed volleyball game is underway and a circle of senior citizens is doing the Hokey Pokey. No joke.

The students in Juan's class listen intently as Augie, their amiable, gray-haired instructor, introduces the night's lesson. "Tonight we're going to take a compression reading on a V-6 engine," he explains as his right hand accentuates the last few syllables. "For those of you who don't know, V-6 means there are three cylinders on each side." Juan, who at 16 looks to be the youngest of the group, nods his head confidently. He already knows that.

For now at least, this cinder-block garage is school for Juan: twice a week, 6 until 9 p.m. Not that he doesn't like it. During his brief career at Thurber High School, auto shop had been one of Juan's favorite courses. He saw it as a natural progression from bicycle repairing and rebuilding, a hobby he had picked up from his father at the age of nine. But at 16, Juan wants more. Fixing cars is fun, but it doesn't fill the void he has felt since leaving Thurber for good in December of his freshman year. After 18 months away from school, he yearns for a return to the classroom, even though as a child it was an atmosphere that had often made him feel claustrophobic. He had hated it when his 4th-grade teacher had forced him to stand up and read an entire 15-page story to his class as punishment for talking too much. He had wanted to break away, to escape, to be "20,000 feet away from her." But compared to life on the streets, Juan says, even that teacher doesn't seem so bad. "And most teachers at Quincy [elementary school] were a lot nicer than her anyway," Juan tells me. "Most of my teachers there taught me good. They were straight."

Thurber High School, on the other hand, was anything but "straight" as far as Juan was concerned. To hear him tell it, the school was literally overrun by gangs, with at least three—the Latin Jesters, the Chi-Town Players, and the Maniac Devils, or MDs—present in heavy numbers. Many of Juan's close friends, knowing the situation that awaited them at Thurber, had become Jesters the summer after graduating from Quincy. While Juan maintains that he didn't "turn," his time at Thurber taught him that perception is sometimes more important than reality. Members of other gangs frequently saw him walking to school and hanging out with kids who were Jesters or Lady Jesters. He sat with them in class and in the lunchroom. In the eyes of the Players and the MDs, it didn't matter whether or not Juan was a full-fledged Jester. He was guilty by association, and this made Juan's life at school increasingly difficult. After a run-in with a group of MDs, he decided that continued attendance at Thurber would constitute a serious risk to his health. Concerned for his safety, he quit, following a path traversed by many neighborhood kids before him— Jesters and non-Jesters alike.

A year and a half later, Juan is still troubled by his flight from high school. He's certain he made the right decision by leaving Thurber—under the circumstances, he doesn't see how he could have done otherwise—but he wants to redeem himself by continuing his education elsewhere. But as is the case for many Back of the Yards teens who drop out and later have second thoughts, his options are few. He was turned down by one school because of poor attendance during his days at Thurber. Another school put him on a long waiting list. And the high schools in his district are out of the question—they're simply not safe places for Juan to be. His latest hope is an alternative high school he heard about one night on a TV news report.

Sitting in his family's apartment the morning after his auto mechanics class, Juan and his mother gather his school records and paperwork for an afternoon interview there.

> *JUAN:* In high school, I was marked up as a Jester 'cause I hung out with them. Everywhere I went I was marked up as a Jester. And I was scared to walk the halls. I never knew if somebody was gonna come up and hit me from the back, or what. It was like each gang had their own floor. I mean, it was their floor, nobody else's. They were the ones that took care of that floor, that's where they hung out, that's where all their lockers were. If you got assigned a locker on a different floor, you changed it to your floor.
>
> They would always be fighting—the Jesters, the Players, and the MDs. And I would back up Tino [a buddy from the neighborhood] and them a hundred percent. They're my friends, you know? They live down the block. And friends are forever, that's the way I see it. So when they would fight, I would usually be there. And I'd be, like, stunned. It'd be two big crowds of guys running against each other, or one crowd chasing the other. Right down the halls, right in the middle of school. And the security guards couldn't do nothing about it.
>
> I think the teachers could've got involved more than they did. I had one cool teacher, my division teacher, Mr. Hastings. He would help you out, he'd always be positive, never negative. But most teachers would just ignore the kids they thought were gangbangers. But if a teacher knows a kid is a gangbanger, they should be teaching him *more*, being near him *more*. That's the person that needs help. The way I see it, a teacher isn't there just to teach. It's like a second guardian for the kid.
>
> One day I was sitting in division and this MD starts telling all these other MDs that I said "MD killer." There was at least ten MDs in there. All of a sudden, they all come up to me and he says, "I heard you said 'MD killer.'" And I said, "I didn't say nothing." 'Cause I didn't. What would I be saying that for? So he goes, "Jester killer! Jester killer!" And I got smart with him, 'cause he had gotten smart with me. So he's like, "We're gonna get this guy," and he showed me his hand and he had a knife. My mouth just dropped.

When the bell rang, I just walked out of the school and I never went back. I told my ma about it, and she went up there to complain, but they didn't do nothing.

So now I'm not in school. And my little brother, he'll see me, and sometimes he'll tell my mother, "I don't wanna go to school." And I tell him, "Hey, I want you to go to school. You'll miss out on a lot of things." I tell him straight up. I lecture him. And I'm the one that should be getting lectured. Here I am not going to school and I'm telling him to go. But that's one reason I want to get back in school somewhere. I want to be a better example for him. 'Cause he looks up to me. Everything that I do, he always wants to be like me. But I tell him not to. I mean, that's my little brother and I wouldn't want anything to happen to him. Sometimes he'll be at the corner store, just standing on the corner, and I'll tell him, "What the fuck is your problem? What are you doing on the corner? Go home!" Or I'll give him some money so he could go in and play video games and stay off the corner. I guess that's why he's always on the corner now, so I'll see him and give him money and he can go play video games.

I tell him exactly what my dad told me when I was a kid. If you ever join in a gang, I'll cut your balls off. But I try to be positive with him, too. I ask him if he did his homework and I ask him about what he's doing in school. I mean, it seems like just yesterday he was a little baby. And I look at him now, and I'm like, "You grew. Time flew. Time flew."

I've been out of school for a year and a half. I'm getting sick and tired of just sitting in the house. I'm not working. I can't find a job. I go ride around on my bike, but, you know, I don't want to go too far. It's dangerous. Around here it's safer, but sometimes the cops mess with us. There's a couple of good cops who tell us, "Hey, get off the corner." That's their job, they gotta do that. But some of them go around abusing people, beating people up for any stupid reason. I know people in the neighborhood want the cops to be strict, but they also don't want them going around beating up their kids. Me and Jose Laredo were getting some gas the other day, and this cop looks at Jose and says, "I should come over there and knock your fucking teeth out, you fucking prick." Then the cop jumped out of his car and started punching Jose through the window. His window was down, and the cop is like, "Come here you motherfucker." He goes, "Get the fuck out of the car." He made us sit on the hood and take our shoes off, 'cause he was searching us. Then he smacked Jose a couple of times, and he's like, "Get the fuck outta here." We got his badge number and everything. We reported him. But we never got a call back.

It's hard to say this, but I miss school. I want to grow up already, I want to be smart. I'll be hearing people talk about different things, about this and that, and I'll be like, "Oh, you learned that in school?" And I'll just feel, like, "Duh." I hate it when people ask me, "Do you go to school?" I just mumble something. I can't even say it. And they'll be like, "Oh, you dropped out." And I'll go, "I didn't drop out, all right? It's just—a little vacation." That's what I tell them. And they're like, "Okay, whatever. You dropped out."

I'll look at my autograph book from eighth grade, and a couple tears will roll down my face, 'cause of all the memories, you know? And every single person that wrote in my autograph book, every single one, wrote: "Don't drop out. Don't drop out. Stay in school." I look at that, and I'm like . . . what happened?

Chapter 8

Some Kind of Justice

When Father Bruce Wellems asked me to help facilitate a weekly gathering of young men in Back of the Yards, the South Side neighborhood where I taught, he wasn't sure exactly what form the meetings would take. "What I know is that these guys need a time to reflect, a place to come together with caring adults," Bruce told me.

Many of the young men he hoped to attract to the group had dropped out of school and were spending a lot of time on the streets. Most were gang members—some more involved than others—and in their teens or early twenties. A few were on probation or recently released from prison. Several had been students of mine back when they were in grammar school.

Bruce suggested we start by introducing the guys to readings that would help them think about their lives, so I brought in articles or short stories I thought might speak to their experiences. And week after week, we read—taking turns, round-robin style. At the end of each session we'd have pizza.

In the beginning it was slow going. Many of the fellas who came to the sessions had been out of school for several years, so just getting through a passage with any sort of narrative flow intact was sometimes a struggle. And once we'd made it through several pages, the discussion didn't exactly flow freely. Bruce or I might talk about themes we saw in the piece, or highlight particular sections we thought were interesting, but the guys often didn't add much to the conversation.

"So what'd you think of the story?" Bruce would ask.

"Straight," someone would inevitably say, and other heads would nod, just barely, to show their approval.

As the weeks and months went by, we continued meeting. Some nights five guys would show up; other nights we'd have twenty-five. Whatever the number, we kept reading, and gradually the discussions began to open up.

Guys started sharing with one another, reflecting on their situations, talking about their futures and the conditions of their communities.

One Tuesday night the topic of discussion was justice, and Porfi[1] got things started. "The cops around here take advantage of their badge," he said. "They push people around."

The first year I taught in the neighborhood, Porfi had been a floppy-haired 6th-grader in my reading class. Back then he read books about Houdini and wanted to be a magician. At 20, his head was shaved close and he talked about one day becoming a cop. And a good cop, too, he was quick to point out. Not like the ones he knew.

He continued: "The cops look at us and they think, 'You're a gang-banger, you ain't got no goals. You ain't gonna be nobody in life. You belong in jail.' So they try to lock us up for any kinda reason."

Around the circle, heads nodded in agreement. The fellas understood. And from the outside looking in, so did I. But I didn't always.

* * *

When I began teaching in Chicago's public schools, my view of gangs was pretty simple. I saw it as me against them. I believed I was in direct competition with street gangs for the minds and souls of the children I taught. It was, to me, a classic scenario of good guys versus bad, and there was no middle ground.

But a couple veteran teachers showed me what I was missing with this hard-line attitude. I was failing to distinguish between the institution of gangs and the individual kids who found protection, respect, and even love within their ranks.

So I began to look more deeply. Slowly, my guard came down. The better I got to know my gang-affiliated students—reading their essays, talking with them during lunch periods, playing basketball together—the less I saw them as some amorphous group called "gangbangers" and the more I saw them as individuals. Jontrell and Ronnie. Junior and Khan. Levon and Tim.

These were the same kids who'd proudly counted off the hundredth day of school as kindergartners; who'd sung corny songs in third-grade assemblies; who'd constructed homemade electric circuits for their 6th-grade science fair project. They were gang members, yes. But they were also our children.

Of course, it's hard to see gang kids as our children—or as anybody's children, really—when they're portrayed only as violent thugs or "super-predators." The gang label has become a sort of code word, a quick and easy answer for what's gone wrong in urban neighborhoods—even in the country as a whole.

But as I observed my students over the years, I came to see gangs more as effect than as cause. Kids like Porfi looked around their communities and saw shuttered factories, abandoned storefronts, jobless men standing on street corners. Crossing neighborhood boundaries meant getting hard looks or, in some cases, much worse—so their world became smaller, their dreams confined to the space of eight square blocks.

At school, they felt disconnected from the curriculum, and were often labeled as behavior problems or tracked into low-end classes. And even if they toughed it out, if they defied the words of the counselor who said they didn't have what it takes to graduate, they understood only too well that a high school diploma didn't mean what it once did. So when guys like Porfi finally did join a gang, it wasn't always so much a choice as a surrender—an acknowledgment that, in their eyes, there were no better choices left.

                                      ✳ ✳ ✳

Back at our Tuesday night session, the guys continued to recount stories of their mistreatment at the hands of Chicago police. They told of having their faces shoved into snowbanks, flashlights shined down their underwear, their front doors broken down, their cars taken for joyrides—their rights violated in a variety of ways.

"But what does that gotta do with justice, though?" asked Vic, who was 21.

"That's *in*justice, dumb ass!" one of the fellas shot back.

"So what is justice?" Father Bruce asked, trying to steer a more productive course.

"There's so much injustice in the world that it's hard to notice any justice," Vic said. "You live all your life not knowing justice, so you get used to not having any at all."

Father Bruce reminded Vic that after a recent shooting in the neighborhood, Vic went after the perpetrators in his car. "You went *looking* for justice," Bruce told him.

"Yeah, because if I can't get it from the police, I'm gonna get my own justice, y'know? And even if it means doing something bad—there's some kind of justice in there somewhere." The look on Vic's face said that he wanted desperately to believe this. Still, he seemed to sense that the notion of justice as revenge wasn't wholly satisfying.

We talked some more, trying to arrive at some sort of consensus, but we never got there. What became clear, though, was that the guys didn't really think about justice in philosophical or abstract terms. For them, it was about the concrete, the lived experience, the day-to-day. And while they clearly understood the principle of leveling the scales, of making things right, they mistrusted the system that was supposed to make it happen. "People talk about 'liberty and justice for all,' " concluded Vic, "but it's not really like that no more."

A few minutes later, the fellas bowed their heads, and Father Bruce led the group in prayer. As the guys called out the names of friends or family members who were locked up, I looked around the circle and asked myself a question I'd asked many times before: Why do they come each week? The free pizza doesn't hurt, but it can't be just that. What is it that keeps them coming back?

What I came to believe is that the guys were searching for something. They sensed that a lot had gone wrong in their lives, and they admitted that they'd made some poor choices, that they'd caused pain to themselves and others. But they also knew that a lot of their suffering was not of their own doing. So the question became one of how to right the wrongs.

For Porfi, Vic, and the rest of the fellas, part of the answer seemed to be that they showed up on Tuesdays. They tried to face their anger and talk about their struggles and their fears. It was a small action, maybe, and in the big picture it may not seem like much. But they were doing something—in this case, something good. And I think Vic was right. There's some kind of justice in there somewhere.

Chapter 9

Ground Zero

My friend Mara was sitting in the reception area of a small Catholic school on Chicago's North Side, where she'd come to inquire about registering her daughter for the upcoming term. She wasn't sure she'd be able to afford the school's monthly tuition bills, but she'd decided to check things out anyway—ask a few questions, pick up some forms, maybe even begin the application process.

The principal, a pleasant, conservatively dressed woman of about 50, welcomed Mara and then quickly ran through her sales pitch, emphasizing the school's small classes and exemplary level of parent involvement. She explained that Mara would be expected to put in her share of volunteer hours, then buzzed through basic information about student uniforms, tuition payment plans, and disciplinary procedures. "Oh yes," she added, pulling a piece of paper from a file folder and handing it to Mara. "You'll also need to sign this."

Mara took the form and glanced at it. At the top of the page, in capital letters, it read "Zero-Tolerance Agreement."

"All of our parents have to sign it," the principal said. "When you read it over, you'll see that it's a first-strike-you're-out situation. That means first offense—no discussion, no excuses."

Mara looked back up at the principal, taken aback by the conversation's sudden change in tone.

"We haven't had any complaints about the policy," continued the principal, perhaps noting the confusion on Mara's face. "The parents all think it's a good thing. With all the school shootings lately, we just . . ." Her voice trailed off. "Well, we just don't want to take any chances."

Mara scanned the list of offenses that could result in a student's swift and automatic expulsion—weapon possession, drug use, gang activity, fighting. But all she could think about was that her daughter was only five years old.

* * *

I don't think I'd ever heard the phrase "zero tolerance" when I began teaching in Chicago Public Schools. That was before Paducah, before Jonesboro, before Littleton. But even before school shootings became a too-familiar item on nightly newscasts, the idea that schools were dealing with a frightening new breed of violent, amoral youth was beginning to take hold. Media reports of rising crime rates played alongside stories of drive-by shootings, gang-related murders, and children killing children. During my first year in the classroom I remember listening to an older colleague's running commentary as she read a magazine article about youth violence. "These kids get worse every year," she said, shaking her head. "They'd just as soon shoot you as look at you."

It was in this climate of fear—some of it justifiable, some not—that zero-tolerance policies began to be seen as a reasonable response to school safety concerns. Proponents argued that the measures would make educators' jobs easier by providing a clear framework for handling serious disciplinary cases. They said schools would be safer because students who caused problems would be removed and other students would be deterred from engaging in violent or criminal activity. Critics countered that zero-tolerance policies would unfairly target students of color, who already often faced stiffer punishments than their White counterparts for similar offenses. But proponents insisted the policies would be fair—there would be no ambiguity. If kids messed up, they were out. Period.

It didn't take long for the idea to gain momentum, and soon it was appearing frequently in the speeches and policy statements of school board members, politicians, and district administrators across the country. Parent groups also jumped on the bandwagon, circulating petitions and doing grassroots organizing. To many, zero tolerance made perfect sense. After all, what teacher doesn't want his job to be a little less stressful? What parent doesn't want her child's school to be as safe as possible? What student doesn't want to receive the same treatment as her peers?

As a new teacher struggling to keep my head above water, I didn't pay much attention to these early rumblings. Not that I didn't think it was an important issue. I'd been as bombarded by media stories as the next person, and there were times—inside and outside of the classroom—when I felt the paranoia creeping in. But I was more worried about getting

LeShawn to come to school and getting Jason to pick up a book than about hypothetical situations involving weapons or drugs. I knew there was a real possibility that I might someday have to confront such a circumstance, but I guess I figured I'd cross that bridge if I came to it. I came to it about 2 months into my 3rd year as a teacher.

* * *

The tardy bell had just rung at Quincy Elementary, a mammoth 100-year-old building in a mostly Mexican-American neighborhood known as Back of the Yards. I was at my third-floor hall-duty post, a blur of middle schoolers blowing past me in both directions. I said hello to passing kids, a little preoccupied because I had only sketchy plans for my first-period class, which began in 10 minutes, but otherwise feeling pretty good given that it was Monday morning. Then up walked Julio.

Lumbering, baby-faced, and—to use his understated self-descrip-tion—"kinda chunky," Julio was an 8th-grader who liked school a lot more than it liked him. He'd had little official academic success during his elementary career, but he showed up every day seemingly undeterred—cheerful, eager to learn what he could, ready to give it his best shot one more time. I didn't know him that well, but I sensed that he was a kid with a huge and generous heart.

"Hey, Michie," he said, reaching out a hand to shake mine, as he often did. He was carrying a dirt-smudged gym bag in the other.

"Morning," I answered, grasping his pudgy palm.

He glanced over his shoulder, then looked down the hall in the other direction. It was almost empty. "I need a favor," he said.

"OK," I replied.

"It's a big one," he said, a hint of worry showing on his face. "A real big one."

"OK. What is it?"

"But you can't tell nobody," he said, grabbing his gym bag with both hands. "I mean, I don't wanna get in trouble. I don't wanna get kicked out."

As far as I knew, Julio had never been in trouble for anything, not even minor rule bending, so I couldn't imagine why he thought he was at risk of getting booted out of school. I motioned him into my classroom.

"I need you to hold my bag for me," he said in hushed tones. "Just till the end of the day."

"OK. You wanna tell me why?"

"Um, well, it's uh," he stammered. "I brought something to school I wasn't supposed to bring."

I relaxed. I'd dealt with this one before: A kid brings some sort of technically against-the-rules but really not such a big-deal piece of contraband to school, suddenly is fearful of being discovered, and wants me to stash it for the day. I wondered what Julio wanted me to hold for him. A tape with explicit lyrics? A pack of cigarettes? A hand-me-down copy of *Playboy*?

I asked to see what he had, and he partially unzipped the gym bag, pulling it open at one end. I peered inside and saw the unmistakable butt of a rifle.

I could hardly believe it. A gun? Contrary to popular belief, there wasn't a .22 in every desk and a knife in every backpack in Chicago public school classrooms. This was the first time I'd seen an actual weapon in school, and I had no idea how to handle the situation. I had no precedent to fall back on, no well of experience to draw from, nothing from my teacher education courses that seemed relevant. I knew that the Board of Education had a detailed "uniform discipline code" that spelled out five categories of student misconduct and a range of disciplinary options for each. I'd never used the code, but I'd looked at it enough times to know that weapon possession was a Group 5 offense, the most severe—a minimum of 6 to 10 days' suspension and a maximum of arrest and expulsion. I remembered a clause buried somewhere in the document that mentioned mitigating circumstances, but I also remembered stories of kids getting suspended for possessing objects that fit the definition of a weapon far less neatly than a gun—nail files, box cutters, Exacto knives.

All of this spun through my head in a matter of seconds, but it didn't help me figure out what to do. Relying on instinct—or maybe just stalling for time—I started asking questions.

Julio told me that it was a BB gun and that it wasn't loaded, though he had a box of BBs in the bag as well. He said he'd been visiting his uncle in the suburbs over the weekend and that he'd used his gym bag as a makeshift suitcase. His uncle liked to hunt, so Julio had taken along the BB gun, hoping the two might get in some target practice, though that didn't happen. He'd come home from his uncle's late Sunday night, woken up late for school, thrown on some clothes as fast as he could, and rushed out the door to beat the late bell. He pointed to his crazily cowlicked hair as evidence. It wasn't until he was inside the school that he'd remembered the gun.

I had no doubt that he was telling the truth. And it was obvious that he had no intention of using the gun, that he wasn't plotting any sort of attack, that bringing it to school was a complete accident. He wouldn't have told me about it otherwise.

So what did I do? I took the bag, locked it up in my closet, talked with Julio about the seriousness of the situation, and made him promise never to make such a mistake again. I returned the bag to him at the end of the day, watched him leave with it, and—until years later—never breathed a word of it to anyone. I had some further conversations with him about the dangers of guns and the risks involved with gun ownership, but other than that, nothing more ever came of the incident.

✳ ✳ ✳

Julio graduated from eighth grade that June, scraping by with Ds in almost every subject, and went on to high school. I didn't think much more about the incident until several years later, when I read a news account about an 11-year-old student in Redwood City, California, who'd accidentally brought an unloaded BB gun to class. By this time Congress had passed the Gun-Free Schools Act—which mandated that any student caught with a firearm on campus be expelled—and school boards across the country had embraced zero tolerance as an all-purpose, get-tough, commonsense solution to school safety problems. The boy in California was an honor student and had never been in trouble of any kind, but he was expelled from his elementary school under its zero-tolerance policy for his entire 6th-grade year.

I flashed back to that morning with Julio and began wildly second-guessing myself. What if another kid had somehow got the gun out of my closet? What if on the way home Julio had decided to show off the gun and had accidentally shot someone? What if he'd been emboldened by my inaction and had shown up with a real gun later in the year? I knew I hadn't handled the situation perfectly. It was poor judgment not to tell any other adult at school what happened, and I could have been more thorough in my follow-up. But the more I thought about the situation and my response to it, the more I was sure I'd done the right thing. Maybe I should have worked out some sort of creative punishment—have Julio do a project on gun violence or arrange for a guest speaker on the topic—but what good would it have done to suspend him or arrest him or expel him for a year? It wouldn't have made our school a safer place, it wouldn't have sent any message to the other students that they didn't already know, and it sure wouldn't have helped Julio.

But in many other zero-tolerance cases around the country, those factors didn't seem to enter the equation. Blind adherence to rules was winning out over doing what was in the best interest of children. Kids were being suspended or expelled for things like sharing a cough drop or a Midol capsule, bringing a steak knife to cut a piece of lunch-box chicken, or displaying a one-inch-long pocketknife during show-and-tell.

Even more troubling than the absurdity of the punishments in these instances was the willingness of adults in positions of authority to abdicate responsibility. Don't blame us, the administrators and school board members seemed to say. Our hands are tied; there's nothing we can do. It was an easy out. And that, I realized, had been part of the appeal of zero tolerance from the beginning: the promise of a simple solution to a tough and complex problem.

Maybe that was why I hadn't been completely turned off by zero-tolerance proposals at first. Like most new teachers, I was still halfheartedly searching for magic pills—instructional methods that would work with every student, classroom-management techniques that would never fail. Deep down, I sensed that one-size-fits-all approaches were unrealistic, yet on the days when I felt my classroom was like a torpedoed ship—which were many—I found myself looking for quick fixes. But the longer I taught, the clearer it became that one size didn't fit all. There was no one way to teach reading effectively, no single method of motivating students, no perfect way to bring history lessons to life. And as much as some educators might have wished it were otherwise, the same went for questions of discipline and school safety.

* * *

One year the week before Thanksgiving, Armando, a 17-year-old former student, came by my house to visit. He told me he'd been suspended from his South Side high school yet again, this time for cutting class. "Man, I'm sick and tired of that," he said. "I mean, they're just dropping kids like it's nothing. Sometimes my teacher takes a kid to get written up, and she'll come back and say to us, 'OK, who's next? I'll suspend you for five days right now!' If teachers want kids to do better, why do they suspend them? They should be keeping them in school, not kicking them out. The guy in the detention room, he tells us, 'If you're doing so bad in school, why do you even bother to come?' Sometimes you feel like they don't even want you there."

The zero-tolerance policy the Chicago Public Schools adopted—which covered kindergarten through the 12th grade—had a dramatic impact in its first 3 years. According to Board of Education figures published at the time, student suspensions system-wide increased more than 51% (from 34,307 to 51,873) during this period and expulsions jumped from 21 to 668—an increase of over 3,000%. But as usual, the numbers told only part of the story. While CPS's written zero-tolerance policy targeted violent and drug-related offenses, more and more students like Armando, who had no such marks on his record, found themselves kicked out for far less serious transgressions—excessive tardiness, skipping class, and failing to wear a student ID were a few of the most common. The uniform discipline code also allowed schools to suspend students for up to five days for repeated violations of catchall infractions such as "failing to abide by school rules" and "defying the authority of school personnel."

Critics of the Board of Education charged that schools were intentionally pushing students out in an effort to improve test scores. The central office denied the allegations, insisting that keeping students in school was a top priority. But while the board had initiated some legitimate efforts to curb the perennially high dropout rate, it had also turned up the heat on administrators to raise standardized test scores by any means necessary. Principals, fearing the threat of probation or school reconstitution, seemed to feel less of an incentive to hold on to kids who might be considered "problems." If those kids weren't in class, their low scores couldn't drag down the school's averages.

Once they were on the streets, it usually wasn't long before they got arrested for one petty offense or another, usually loitering. If schools had zero tolerance, some of the cops who worked in the community seemed to have even less. "All this neighborhood is," a White officer visiting my school once told me, "is one big gang." That sentiment wasn't lost on the young people who lived in the area.

It was disheartening, to say the least, to watch so many of my students graduate from 8th grade and then get pushed out of high school only to wind up on the streets or locked up. I knew most of these guys well enough to see that, although they'd made some poor choices, they still had plenty of potential. What they needed was another chance.

∗ ∗ ∗

Soon after arriving at school one February morning, I learned that a student in my reading class, a 12-year-old, had been arrested the previous evening for the murders of two teenagers. He'd been serving a week-long suspension for drawing gang signs in his notebook—the final straw in a series of run-ins he'd had with teachers and administrators over the previous several months. I'd visited the boy's house the previous afternoon, just hours before the shootings, to take him some assignments and a book to read. I found it hard to believe he'd committed the crime, but according to the police, witnesses said he got out of a car just after 6:30 p.m., walked up to the two other boys, and fired several shots at them point-blank. He tried to run, but a squad car caught up to him a block or so away. Once handcuffed and in the car, police said, he confessed to the killings.

For the next few days my classroom was crawling with reporters, and the story was front-page news in the *Chicago Tribune* and at the top of nightly newscasts. The coverage was often sensationalized—a headline in the *Salt Lake City Tribune* read "Double Murder Halts Career of Chicago Gangster, 12." I could see zero-tolerance supporters using the case as evidence of why such harsh measures were necessary. They could argue that it was a good thing the accused student was suspended at the time of the shooting—just imagine what might have happened had he been in school that day.

But some people saw the shootings as evidence that inflexible disciplinary policies weren't working. One of them was Father Bruce Wellems, a priest at Holy Cross Church, which sits directly across the street from Quincy. He saw the killings as a wake-up call, a clear sign that something needed to be done, but he was looking for a better solution. "With something like zero tolerance, you're not dealing with the problem," he says. "You're not facing what the issues really are. It's like the Ten Commandments—'Thou shalt not, thou shalt not, thou shalt not.' OK, but what *will* you do? What's the other side of that?"

Born and raised in Albuquerque, Wellems came to Chicago in the early 1980s to study for the priesthood. He landed at Holy Cross in 1991 with only a vague idea of what an inner-city ministry might look like and little commitment to the neighborhood's struggling youth. "I remember Tim McGovern, who was the park supervisor at the time, working with some of the gang kids, taking them on trips," Wellems says. "He'd always try to get me to come along, but I really didn't want to get into it. I was afraid. I kept trying to turn away from them, and Tim would keep turning me back again. One day we were at the park and I said, 'Tim, you know, these gang kids are really bad kids, they're really dangerous.' And I'll never forget what Tim told me. 'Bruce,' he said, 'these gang kids are your kids.' And he was right. They are our kids."

Wellems started working extensively with dropouts and gang members in the community, and he quickly discovered that most of them wanted one of two things—a decent job or the chance to continue their education. But finding schools that would accept the kids was hard, and keeping them enrolled was even harder—especially after zero tolerance became the rule.

When Eddie, a 14-year-old who'd recently dropped out, was shot in a drive-by, he asked Wellems to help him get back into school. Wellems got him enrolled in a Catholic high school, and Eddie sailed through 9th grade until the final month, when a teacher caught him scribbling gang graffiti on a desk. In short order, he was expelled and given no credit for the course work he'd completed. Wellems tried to intervene, but the principal wouldn't budge. "We don't tolerate gang activity," the principal said. "That's our rule, and we follow our rules."

Fine, Wellems thought. If other schools don't want to help these kids, I'll start my own. He'd tossed around the idea of a community high school before but hadn't known how to get the right people behind it. When the city's attention turned to Back of the Yards in the wake of the two murders, he decided to try to use it to make something good come out of the tragedy. In late February, then-CEO of Chicago Public Schools Paul Vallas visited Quincy, and Wellems tagged along on the tour, championing the idea of an alternative school at every opportunity. By the end of the morning, Vallas had made a verbal commitment.

Launching the high school became Wellems's mission. He decided to call it the Sister Irene Dugan Alternative High School after a Religious of the Cenacle nun who'd worked with some of the neighborhood's gang members during the last year of her life. "Irene always used to tell me, 'Bruce, teach them to read,'" he says. "And that really made sense to me—the importance of learning to read. It does so many things. It raises their self-awareness, their awareness of what's going on around them, what they know, what they're able to know. And as they come to an appreciation of that, they calm down, they grow."

In the months that followed, Wellems formed a coalition of neighborhood educators, business leaders, community activists, and volunteers who worked together to map out details and build support. He visited alternative schools in Los Angeles to gather ideas about scheduling, curriculum, and encouraging parental involvement. Every Tuesday night he, counselor Sergio Grajeda, and I met with a group of 15 to 20 guys who were interested in signing up for the school—getting their input, keeping the momentum going.

As the weeks passed, Wellems cleared or kicked aside hurdle after hurdle, and by August Dugan Alternative School was up and running. Housed in a small brick building on the back lot of Holy Cross that had once been used as overflow classroom space for Quincy, the school opened with 19 students, many of whom had police records or were gang members. Several had been pushed out of other schools, often for minor offenses. "Society can say they won't tolerate this type of individual, and so can schools," Wellems says. "But what does that do? It makes the kid feel rejected. They're in a corner, and they give up. They're back out on the street affecting ten other kids in a negative way. How does a kid have room to screw up and grow when you have something like zero tolerance? How about having a kid atone for something? How is there any atonement if you just flat out reject a kid?"

In the media and in our imaginations, kids—especially city kids—have become the scapegoats for our own worst misdeeds. But examined more closely, this is clearly a distorted view. Urban children, particularly youth of color, are often under attack. Whether it's zero-tolerance measures or cuts in funding for arts programs or anti-bilingual education crusades or the exclusive use of biased standardized tests to evaluate student progress, city kids—particularly African Americans and Latinos—are suffering. The question we must ask ourselves is: How will we respond?

"The ills of this society affect all of us, and it takes all of us to work together to do something about them," Wellems says. "We can try to blindfold ourselves to it or try to turn away from the kids who need our help, but they're not going away. We turn away because we're afraid to know them. But once you make the effort to get to know them, what you find is a lot of life in these guys. I really believe some of our best leaders are going to come from these kids."

Chapter 10

A Real Alternative

Tragedy and Hope on Chicago's South Side

On a cold November morning, 18-year-old Uvaldo hunches over a wooden desk at Irene Dugan Alternative High School and scribbles his name on a sign-in sheet. "Morning, Ms. B.," he says to Norine Baltazar, the school's parent liaison.

"Right on time," I say, thinking Uvaldo has slipped in just before the school's 10:00 a.m. start.

"No, he's a minute late," says Baltazar, glancing at a wall clock. "And by the time he gets up to class it'll be two minutes. Late is late." Uvaldo cocks his head, his expression somewhere between a grin and a grimace.

Baltazar smiles. "And take off the hat," she adds as Uvaldo heads up the stairs to the second floor, where he and eleven other teenagers will soon be engaged in a spirited discussion of Aldous Huxley's *Brave New World*.

Uvaldo enrolled at Dugan after leaving a traditional high school because he felt unsafe. Other students have their own stories. Tony was ordered to attend an alternative school after repeated suspensions—once for being caught on school grounds with two ounces of marijuana. Karina was arrested and advised not to return to her high school after taking part in a lunchroom fight with another girl. Manuel can't point to a specific reason things didn't work out at his former school. "I just stopped going," he tells me. "Over there they don't really care if you go or not."

Whatever the causes, these young people—along with about four dozen other students at Dugan—all left their assigned high schools before graduating. Citywide, they have lots of company. Though official dropout rates for Chicago Public Schools (CPS) dipped slightly from 2000 to 2005, the numbers remain alarmingly high—especially if you follow the same group of students over time. A study by the Consortium on Chicago

School Research, which tracked CPS students from age 13 to 19, put the cohort dropout rate at 41.7% in 2004.[1]

And the problem isn't limited to Chicago. Nationwide, U.S. students in large urban systems have a graduation rate of just 57.5%.[2] Because the students in many big-city school systems are predominantly poor, African American, and/or Latino/a, these groups are affected disproportionately by low graduation/high dropout rates, and the social consequences are devastating. What's worse, the dropout/push-out numbers may be on the rise. Numerous reports from across the United States suggest that struggling schools, desperate to raise test scores to meet their Adequate Yearly Progress (AYP) goals mandated by the No Child Left Behind Act, are committing educational triage by pushing out low-achieving students.[3]

Dugan opened following the killing of two neighborhood teenagers by a 12-year-old who was, at the time, one of my 7th-grade students.[4] In an effort to help the community heal from the tragedy, a local priest, Father Bruce Wellems, galvanized an effort to open a small alternative high school that would serve the area's most vulnerable youth. Among the schools' initial enrollees was 21-year-old Federico Vega, who became Dugan's first valedictorian the following June. He had been suspended for fighting at the beginning of his senior year and had given up on returning to school until Dugan opened its doors.

"My life has changed a lot in this past year," he said in his commencement speech. "If I could turn back time I would change all of the negative choices I made in my life, and I would trade them with positive ones. But as you all know, that is impossible to do. I can't change the past, but I can change my future. I can learn from my mistakes and change my ways. I think all of us can."

* * *

Nine years and over 100 graduates later, Federico's message continues to echo in Dugan's classrooms. Chela, an 18-year-old who quit school and turned to drugs after her father succumbed to bone cancer when she was in 8th grade, credits Dugan's staff with helping her get a fresh start. She's been off drugs for two years, and she's on track to become the first in her family to finish high school. "I used to have real low self-esteem," Chela says. "But ever since I came here all the teachers have been supporting me a lot. One of my teachers takes me home from school sometimes. They helped me get a job. They set my family up with a counselor. They notice right away when something's wrong."

Like Chela, most teenagers—even those who outwardly resist school, even kids in gangs—want to feel connected to, and supported by, caring adults. But in too many oversized, traditional high schools, a "crisis of relationships"[5] exists that leads young people to feel disconnected. Pedro Noguera[6] interviewed and observed students at ten Boston high schools and found that more than half "did not believe that their teachers really cared."[7]

It's not hard to imagine why. While individual teachers in large urban high schools may work valiantly to foster strong relationships with their students, institutional backing for such efforts is often weak. Lacking formal supports, some teachers grow weary of battling school cultures characterized by anonymity. Others never take up the fight. A former 8th-grade student of mine lamented the fact that, halfway through the year at his 2,800-student Chicago high school, his history teacher still didn't know his name.

Dugan's teachers understand this reality, and believe that making personal connections with students, many of whom have felt invisible or alienated at their former schools, is central to their work. Classes are small—the maximum is 15 students—and instructional programs are personalized. "Our success has been about relationships from the beginning, and it still is," says Brigitte Swenson, who has taught at the school since it opened and now serves as its administrative and instructional leader. "Students aren't just numbers here. They're known by every teacher in the school."

That doesn't mean there aren't challenges with individual students. Some kids rebel against attendance policies they believe are too strict. Others struggle to leave behind poor study habits or to reverse what Florence Rubinson has called "a long, slow, and often painful withdrawal from learning."[8] Conflicts among students flare up on occasion. But when problems arise, the strong teacher-student bonds allow staff members to better understand and address the underlying causes, rather than react with punitive, one-size-fits-all responses. When several teachers noticed a student becoming increasingly unmotivated toward academics and antagonistic toward his classmates, the entire staff—all five teachers plus Swenson—sat down with the teen for an extended conversation, both to reaffirm their support for him and to clarify expectations.

Crystal McDonell, who teaches French, appreciates such efforts. "At the other schools where I taught, it was like, 'Read the code of conduct, write them up, send them to the vice principal,'" she says. "But here it's more like, 'Let's talk about it. What's the history with this kid? Let's talk to everybody who's dealt with him and come to a decision about what's best.'" Dugan, McDonell says, has the feel of a family, "and when you screw up with your family, you get another chance."

∗ ∗ ∗

From the beginning, Swenson and Dugan's teachers (along with Father Wellems, who continued to advise the staff) had to think creatively about every detail of the school's operation. Some of the questions they pondered were those likely to be asked at any start-up: How can we help students take ownership of the school? How can we meet the needs of kids who come in at a wide range of readiness levels? What should the curriculum be? Others were quandaries specific to Dugan's size, its student population, or its lack of physical space: How will district requirements for classes like music and physical education be fulfilled? What if kids come to school wearing gang colors? What will students eat for lunch—and where?

Experience, Swenson says, has been the best teacher. While she and her staff continue to retool elements that aren't working, they've learned many lessons about fashioning and sustaining a school that meets troubled kids where they are and challenges them to invest in their own learning. Among them:

- While it's essential that teachers build trusting relationships with students, it is, in itself, not enough. Researcher Michelle Fine, long a supporter of grassroots small school initiatives, says she worries in private "that some small schools substitute caring for serious intellectual growth."[9] Dugan's teachers try to guard against that possibility by tackling stimulating subject matter in required courses and offering electives that help students examine their worlds through different lenses—classes such as Criminal Justice, Chicago Fiction, Film Studies, and Law in American Society. "There's a stigma out there about alternative schools," Swenson says. "That they're places where you try to get kids through the day but not a lot is going on intellectually.

I think our teachers work really hard to have meaningful classes and to push kids to think critically."

- Students who haven't found success in high school—for whatever reason—need to see tangible results as quickly as possible. "There's a need for instant gratification," Swenson says. "If they don't see themselves making progress, they get frustrated." To account for this, Dugan incorporates a block schedule in which students take four 80-minute classes each day. The longer class periods allow students to earn a semester's worth of credit in each course in just nine weeks—credits they can view on a transcript right away. In relatively short order, students begin to see that they can indeed be competent, and even successful, in school—a possibility that is foreign to many Dugan youth. As that realization settles in, students are less likely to feel they are drowning in an "ocean of inadequacy" and more apt to work to develop their "islands of competence."[10]
- Regular attendance and punctuality are often a struggle for students who are returning to school after a prolonged absence, or who attended erratically at their former schools. During its first year Dugan didn't have a strict, formalized attendance policy, and some students took advantage. Now expectations are clear and, except for in extreme situations, non-negotiable: If you miss more than four days in a quarter, you're dropped and have to start again the next marking period. "The kids fight against it," Swenson says, "but we try to approach it as, 'If you're not here, you're not learning.'" And the results are impressive: Dugan's attendance rate—with a student body made up of many youth who have had trouble going to school consistently in the past—is 93%; the average for CPS high schools is 86%.
- The goal is to keep students in school, not put them out, so the flip side of adhering to strict attendance guidelines is doing as much as possible to help kids meet their commitment. In other words, the responsibility of ensuring high attendance rates shouldn't rest entirely on individual students—the school, too, should play a role.[11] One way Dugan does this is with a 10 o'clock start, which allows its teenage clientele to sleep later and still make it to school on time (and also keeps them off the streets during the potentially

dangerous late-afternoon hours). In addition, students who don't show up get a call the same morning—and sometimes a home visit as well—from the school's parent liaison, who tries to troubleshoot and get them to class. For kids who fail to hold up their end of the bargain, redemption is always just around the corner. If a student is dropped for missing too many days, he can always start anew the following quarter. Dugan's year-round schedule allows students to be admitted (or re-admitted) four times each year.

- Small schools shouldn't become islands unto themselves. Connecting with individuals, cultural and arts organizations, businesses, and other resources both inside and outside the immediate community is crucial if alternative education sites are to survive and thrive. In part, this is because improved schooling alone cannot sufficiently address the many social, emotional, medical, economic, and other needs that students who have not succeeded in traditional schools bring with them.[12] At Dugan, Swenson and her staff leverage relationships with parents, parishioners, a neighboring elementary school, probation officers, employers, the police department, private donors, and several arts organizations in an effort to provide students with a richer educational experience, and to offer services and extracurricular options that would otherwise be unavailable in a small school setting.

Of course, there are many lessons yet to be learned at Dugan, and challenges that remain. Perhaps the most important is figuring out how to continue to evolve in an educational universe where top-down mandates and one-size-fits-all "solutions" are the order of the day. In the midst of such an environment, Swenson worries that the freedom Dugan has enjoyed in the past could suddenly be curtailed. "There's always a level of concern that someone's going to see what we're doing and not support it because we do things differently," she says. "It's like we're always looking over our shoulder thinking, 'Are we going to get caught?'"

Lehr and Lange have argued that, in this era of high-stakes accountability, alternative schools need to amass as much quantitative data as possible to bolster their chances of garnering continued funding and support.[13] While that is undoubtedly good advice, it's also true that numbers alone often miss the most important parts of the story. A hundred Dugan graduates over eight years, for example, may seem like a drop in the bucket when weighed against the bigger picture of dropout statistics and the failure of public schools to educate all students.

Yet for many of those hundred, Dugan has been life-changing: a refuge, a second chance, a step along a different, more hopeful journey. Juan had been out of school for nearly 2 years and was heavily involved in gang activity when he enrolled at Dugan. Now 25 and a graduate of the school, he's taking classes toward an associate's degree and working part-time at a downtown Chicago law firm. His dream of attending law school, once distant and fading, now seems legitimately within reach.

The question is not whether young people who've lost their way in traditional schools—kids who've been pushed out or kicked out, who are young mothers, who are lured into gangs—value education. Like Juan and Chela and Federico, most of them clearly do. The real question is whether we value them enough to provide a schooling experience that works for them. After all, reconnecting dropouts, as Nancy Martin and Samuel Halperin point out, "is not rocket science. Rather, it is more an exercise in imagining what might be, of having the skills, the will, and the stamina to shape reality in more creative and positive directions."[14]

Dugan's founders, teachers, and students have spent nearly a decade imagining "what might be" on Chicago's South Side and mustering the necessary will to keep their vision alive. Asked if the efforts have been worthwhile, Swenson's reply comes without hesitation: "There are a hundred kids out there who, before they came here, never thought they were going to finish high school. Is that cost effective? Is it practical? Is it worth it? I say yes, absolutely."

Chapter 11

At the Edges of a Dream

I don't remember ever doubting, as a teenager, whether I would go to college. I assumed I would, and even though money was often tight in our house (my mother kept her budgeted monthly cash allotments in labeled metal Band-Aid boxes in a kitchen cabinet), I didn't worry a lot about how my parents would afford it. I'd heard stories since I was young of my mom waiting tables at her campus dining hall and my dad quarterbacking his small-college football team, so the concept of leaving home at 18 to continue my own education seemed both familiar and natural. Even as early as junior high school, college didn't seem like a distant dream—it was more like another expected step on my path. I knew it wasn't that way for everybody, but at the time I understood only dimly just how much the cards were stacked in my favor.

For the 7th- and 8th-graders I taught in Chicago years later, things were far different. They stood on the other side of the stacked deck, and for some, thinking about going to college was a bit like mulling over a trip to a distant planet. Many of them looked at the evidence around them, in their neighborhood and on TV, and reasoned that college was for other people—rich kids, white kids—not them. After all, even if they worked hard and did well in high school, how would they be able to afford college when their parents were already struggling to get by? And since some were undocumented immigrants, another barrier stood in their way: they wouldn't be eligible for federal loans or work-study jobs to help pay for their collegiate studies.

But thanks to a combination of uncommon resilience, bouyant hope, and perhaps the influence of a family member who had made the post-secondary plunge, a number of students managed to keep their eyes on the college dream. I encouraged them whenever I could, but I also tried not to assume it was the single best path for each of my students. For some youth, pursuing a trade or a passion via a more direct, non-academic route may make more sense. Still, when a research study reports that only eight of every 100 Chicago Public School freshmen earn a bachelor's degree by the time they reach their mid-20s,[1] it's hard to deny that something is terribly wrong, and that far too many low-income students in the city are not getting the educational opportunities they deserve.

So while I tried to support and validate a wide range of possible futures when speaking with my 8th-graders, I pushed the college path, and I was pleased when a handful of former students started getting accepted at local campuses. It didn't take long to be reminded, however, that getting in was only part of the battle. For most, money was a constant worry. I can't count the number of former students who had to discontinue their studies after just two or three semesters when a parent got laid off or couldn't keep up with their tuition payments. Negotiating the racial and cultural realities of their campuses was an equally daunting challenge. Having grown up in a low-income Mexican immigrant community, many found the university climates they encountered to be not only foreign, but intimidating.

Nancy, who I'd taught when she was an 8th-grader, left her family's modest apartment on Chicago's South Side to attend DePaul University in the city's Lincoln Park neighborhood. It was only a 25-minute drive from where she'd grown up, but to Nancy it felt like another world.

> My two brothers drove me there in this old Chevy Cavalier that I'd bought for a hundred dollars. And I remember carrying in my stuff in a milk crate. I didn't have a lot—clothes, sheets, a little black-and-white TV. But the other kids were driving up in big U-Hauls! They were bringing in loads and loads—suitcases full of clothes and huge TVs and stereo systems and real storage bins. I had a milk crate![2]

In her dorm, all of Nancy's suitemates where White, and with the exception of one, none of them had grown up in the city.

> I was like, these are the White people from TV. I could just imagine the way their lives had been—the whole 'I go upstairs to my bedroom' thing. I felt so small, so ashamed. I felt like I stood out. And not just with material things, but with how I dressed, how I spoke. I started questioning all that.[3]

I heard more stories like Nancy's when I left my public school class-room and began teaching undergraduates at a large state university. Both the campus and its surrounding community were overwhelmingly White, with African American and Latino undergraduates combined making up only about 10% of the student population. Not surprisingly, acclimating to this environment wasn't easy for many students of color. In my courses and in one-on-one conversations, I listened as African American and Latino students recounted instances of subtle bias and blatant racism, expressed feelings of marginalization, and shared their frustrations with navigating the "White space"[4] of the university.

Of course, most White undergrads didn't see the campus and com-munity as "White space" at all. From their perspective, the campus cli-mate wasn't racialized, it was neutral—a variation on a norm they had been accustomed to throughout their lives. A White student might walk past a wall of photos of former university presidents or trustees and see it simply as a respectful nod to the school's heritage—not giving a thought to the race of the people (mostly men) in the photos. An African Ameri-can or Latino student, on the other hand, might look at the dozens of White faces and be immediately struck by the notion that almost none of them look like her.[5]

One of my faculty colleagues, Beth Hatt, had engaged in similar con-versations with some of her African American and Latino students. We were both troubled by the lack of racial diversity of campus, not only be-cause of its possible implications regarding the depth of the institution's commitment to equity issues, but because of its potential harmful impact on students of color. When we learned that the graduation rates for Black and Latino students were about half that of Whites and Asians, we grew even more concerned. So we decided to interview some African Ameri-can and Latino undergraduates about their experiences at the school to try to get a better understanding of what was going on from the students' perspectives.[6]

Several students we interviewed noted the limited presence of faculty of color on campus, and recognized this as not merely happenstance, but as a reflection of the university's lack of commitment to recruiting and retaining African American and Latino faculty. They also made connec-tions between this reality and low retention rates among Black and Latino students. Raul, a Mexican American junior, said:

I haven't had any Hispanic professors. Actually I haven't had any Hispanic or African American professors the whole time I've been here. At all. I think it's definitely important to try to recruit more, because it gives students inspiration [and] they might feel a little more comfortable approaching professors.

Many students also talked about how their in-class, academic experiences were impacted by the lack of racial and cultural diversity among the school's faculty and student body. While almost all of the interviewees recalled multiple instances of being "the only one in the class," some students said that, in general, they hadn't felt singled out or mistreated by their professors. But many did recall examples of race-related classroom indignities—uncomfortable, often hurtful moments that Harvard professor Chester Pierce termed "racial microaggressions."[7] These are not blatant, explicit acts but "unconscious and subtle forms of racism."[8] The cut, however, can be just as deep. Kayla, an African American junior studying Business Education, described feeling singled out in a class where she was the only Black student:

> The teacher would just say little comments, like, "Oh, some of you guys might teach in an urban neighborhood," and then she'd look at me. Every time she directed something toward urban issues, she'd look at me. Or people who are different than you, she'd look at me. And I changed my seat one time just to see if she'd keep looking that way—and she still looked at me.

Beyond the walls of the classroom—in the dorms or dining halls, at local stores, or on the streets of the community—many students were reminded that they were still "outsiders" no matter how long they'd been students at the university. These sometimes took the form of microaggressions and other times were acts of unvarnished racism. Nayeli, a Mexican American senior, remembered an incident that occurred outside the campus bookstore:

> I was talking on the phone to my aunt . . . and I was told to learn how to speak English by this guy. He was like [yelling], "Learn how to fucking speak English." And I'm like, "I know how to fucking speak English, alright?" And my aunt's like "Don't be talking like that! Why

are you swearing?" And I'm like, "Because he just told me to learn English." And then she started going off, and I'm like, "Exactly, Tia, this is how it is here."

Taneka, an African American student who was actively involved in a number of campus activities, recalled a hurtful experience that occurred her freshman year when she was volunteering with Habitat for Humanity to help build a house for a needy local family:

> [Another undergrad volunteer came up to me and said], "Oh, I bet you're so glad to be moving into this house." And I was like, "This isn't my house." And she said, "Oh, I thought you lived here," and I said, "No, I don't know them. This is not my house." So that kind of took me aback.

A number of other themes came up in the interviews—aspects of life on a predominantly White campus that made it difficult for students of color. Interviewees talked about the feeling of being under surveillance by campus and local police, a lack of institutional resources devoted to cultural programming or student organizations, and having to struggle for what they believed many White students took for granted. Monique, an African American education major, put it this way:

> It's hard . . . [Y]ou have to fight for resources, you have to fight for acknowledgement, you have to fight for respect amongst your peers who may have never had a class with an African American, or who may have never heard an African American perspective on issues of education or social inequity . . . It's a constant battle. And I think that's what makes going to a predominantly white university so difficult: You're always fighting. It goes beyond just being a student— you're a student with a fight. And that makes the experience a lot more daunting.

Monique was an incredibly resilient and resourceful senior, and had found ways to persevere through the hardships of her college experience. But as the university's retention and graduation rates for students of color showed, many African American and Latino students—the majority, in fact—didn't make it to their commencement day. Kayla reminded us of this when, in her interview, she recalled arriving as a freshman with a group of African American girls from her high school. "Out of the seven of us that came down here together [five years ago], only one has graduated," she said. "Two of us are fifth-year seniors. And the rest of them—gone."

Of course, multiple factors, both personal and institutional, play into whether any student's path to and through college is a successful one. Every student has choices to confront, and most young people make their share of mistakes along the way. But for many African American and Latino youth who grow up in places like Chicago, a confluence of factors largely outside their control conspire to give them fewer options in the first place, and less of an opportunity to rebound if they are tripped up along the way: poverty, inadequate academic preparation, unwelcoming university climates, stalled legislation to assist undocumented students. Given everything that stands in their path—the stacked deck that worked to my advantage but their detriment—I'm more often astounded by how many urban youth do make it to their college graduations, not by how many don't.

That's not a call for complacency—rather, it's an acknowledgment that many young people are doing their part. But they need support—not just from their families and teachers (though that's clearly important), but systemic, institutional efforts: high school counselors who have time to actually provide counsel; greater availability of challenging coursework in their high schools; intensified recruitment outreach from universities; more effective and compassionate support systems once they're on campus; a higher priority on hiring and retaining faculty of color; policies and governmental supports that make college more affordable; and much more.

As it is, we too often line the walls of classrooms in low-income communities with motivational posters and hope for the best:

Success is 99% hard work.
If you believe, you can achieve.
When I let myself dream, anything is possible.

I'm all for inspiration, but I didn't put sayings like those on the walls for my 7th- and 8th-graders to read. It wasn't just that the words are unbearably hokey—more than that, I figured that the kids I taught, most of whom were growing up amid poverty and other adversities, knew that the world was far more complicated than greeting-card slogans could convey.

They understood that hard work matters, but many needed look no further than their own parents to see that hard work alone often wasn't enough to substantially alter one's circumstances. They knew that believing in themselves was important, but at the same time they were left to wonder just how much others believed in them.

Still, many of the students I taught persisted, despite evidence around them that sometimes mocked their devotion. Jose Alonso was a quick-witted 12-year-old with an infectious laugh when he stepped into my Media Studies class years ago. Now 30, he's an attorney—a graduate of Northwestern University and Loyola University's School of Law. He's also chair of the immigration reform committee at Holy Cross, the neighborhood parish, where he works to organize and advocate for undocumented youth. As the middle child of parents who came to the U.S. as immigrants without papers, he understands the students' struggles.

On an overcast Saturday morning in a bare church hall, Jose looks out on a gathering of about thirty young people—most of them undocumented, all of them hoping to pursue a college education and wondering how they'll afford it without a social security number. "We're here today to share our stories, to remember that we're not alone, and to share resources and strategies," Jose says as he kicks off the event. "Your job is to take these resources back to the community."

One by one, the students introduce one another and talk about their varied interests. One enjoys art, another is a cross-country runner, another played the clarinet for seven years, and still another volunteered in New Orleans after Hurricane Katrina. Later, they share details of their immigration experiences. Each walks a singular path, but they share a common bond. "We do different things in life, but we're so similar," one of the students, a high school junior, says later. "And to see the different things people have gone through and the parallel lives—it's amazing."

Amazing indeed. Even more so that these young people aren't giving up. They're joining hands, putting their heads together to strategize, refusing to stay quiet. Uncertain but undaunted, they push on, taking small steps closer to the edges of a dream.

Part III

The Bigger Picture

Chapter 12

Elephants in the Room

City teachers learn to brace themselves whenever a school-related story makes the front page or a website's top headline. The news usually isn't good. In Chicago, where I've worked as a teacher and teacher educator for the past two decades, we've grown accustomed to being pummeled with horror stories about ourselves, our students, and our schools.

Those of us who spend time in the city's classrooms understand that such stories are almost always gross oversimplifications of real-life complexities. We also know that, shock-and-awe headlines to the contrary, there is beauty, hope, and resilience to be found in the communities and buildings in which we work. We just don't expect to hear about it in the mainstream media.

But it's not only the negativity of the coverage of urban schools that's a problem. Equally troubling is the tendency of mainstream outlets to gloss over or bury story threads that actually deserve a screaming headline or an hour-long special report. Indeed, what's often most instructive about splashy, attention-grabbing pieces that focus on urban schools is not what they do mention, but what they don't.

NCLB's Problem? Irresponsible Parents

In 2004 the *Chicago Tribune* published a three-part, front-page special report ostensibly focused on the impact of the No Child Left Behind (NCLB) Act on Chicago's schools.[1] The protagonist of the series was 9-year-old Rayola Carwell. Rayola's mother, Yolanda, had taken advantage of the school-transfer provision of NCLB by pulling her daughter out of a South Side school that the article dubbed "among the worst in the city" and enrolling her at Stockton Elementary, 13 miles from the family's home. Out of nearly 270,000 students who were eligible for transfers citywide, only a handful were actually granted transfers by Chicago Public Schools.

The story that unfolded over three days and ten full *Tribune* pages turned out to be less about a seriously flawed and woefully underfunded educational policy than about perpetuating stereotypes of low-income parents. The spotlight shined not on NCLB, but on Yolanda Carwell, who was described as "a single mother of three who dropped out of high school … [and] spent her life moving from one low-paying job to another." When tardies and absences began to mount for Rayola at her new school and her academic work suffered, Carwell's parenting skills took center stage in the *Tribune*'s narrative.

The article stated that Carwell frequently allowed her children to stay up past midnight watching TV, and when they were too tired to get up, she let them miss school. When Rayola and her siblings got into arguments, readers were told that their mother couldn't hear them because "she [was] upstairs on the phone." We also learned that Carwell had "enrolled in, but not completed, three GED training courses at three different community colleges." Paragraph after paragraph, day after day, the mother's apparent disregard for her children's welfare was underscored.

By the end of the series, which culminated with Rayola leaving Stockton and returning to a school near her home, little attention had been given to the lack of federal funding to help schools address NCLB mandates. Nothing had been said about how the increasing focus on high-stakes accountability measures—intensified under NCLB—handcuffed teachers around the country, especially in big-city systems that serve large numbers of poor and immigrant children. And barely a mention was given to the sheer folly of the transfer provision: When the ground-level reality in Chicago was that schools had only a thousand available spots for 270,000 eligible transferees, wasn't that the big story?

But readers weren't asked to consider any of that—at least not for long. Instead, they were left with the impression that the main thing holding Rayola back from a high-quality education was a negligent mother. And if there was any doubt about coming to that conclusion, a *Tribune* editorial written a few days later hammered the point home. While gingerly criticizing aspects of NCLB, the editorial board reserved its harshest words for Carwell:

Yolanda Carwell had the best of intentions when she took advantage of the No Child Left Behind Act. . . . But good intentions aren't always enough to educate children. . . . Carwell couldn't get her children out of bed early. She wouldn't make them turn off the TV. She couldn't manage to get herself to work and her kids to school. . . . The No Child Left Behind Law has focused welcome attention on a critical issue that schools have long avoided confronting: the achievement gap between minority and non-minority students. . . . [But] no well-intentioned law, no well-intentioned school can succeed without the follow-through of a child's parent.[2]

Just like that, all of us—except for Yolanda Carwell—were let off the hook, absolved from any collective responsibility for the failure of Chicago schools to provide a quality education to children like Rayola. Never mind re-hauling NCLB, the paper's editors seemed to say. What really needs fixing is poor people.

Oprah Examines Educational Inequities—or Not

Insightful reporting probably isn't what most viewers expect from Oprah Winfrey, but I watched her special, "American Schools in Crisis," with an open mind. While Oprah's shameless gushing over celebrity guests can be tiresome, she has also dedicated entire programs to issues that might not otherwise appear on her audience's radar screen: the genocides in Darfur and Rwanda, the AIDS epidemic in Africa, the human toll of Hurricane Katrina. Call me a sucker, but I'm willing to cut her at least a little slack.

The "American Schools in Crisis" special wasn't focused solely on urban schools. But Oprah turned her attention to Chicago in a segment called "Trading Schools," in which camera crews followed two groups of kids—one from Harper High School on the city's South Side and another from Neuqua Valley High School in Chicago's western suburbs—as they visited each other's campuses for a day.

Anyone familiar with the vast inequities that characterize our nation's schools could've guessed what the kids might find, but that didn't make the contrasts captured by Oprah's cameras any less jaw-dropping. At Neuqua Valley, an Olympic-sized swimming pool and a state-of-the-art fitness center. At Harper, a pool that hadn't seen water in ten years and a gym with dilapidated equipment and a leaky ceiling. At Neuqua Valley, an award-winning music department; at Harper, an Instrumental Music class with no instruments. More striking still was the disparity in the schools' core curricular offerings. According to the report, over two dozen advanced placement classes are offered at Neuqua Valley, while Harper has just two.

In a voice-over during the segment, Oprah narrated, "Over and over, [the students] see the glaring inequities between the two schools. It is a harsh lesson that leaves many of the kids asking why." If that's what they were asking, though, the rest of the program did little to help them—or the show's viewers—arrive at any answers. Several of the most significant causes of such educational disparities—state funding formulas that perpetuate abominable monetary gaps between rich and poor districts, persistent residential segregation, and the abandonment of urban public schools by White and middle-class city dwellers—went unmentioned.

Yes, there was a sound bite from author Jonathan Kozol, who unapologetically used the word "apartheid" to describe public schooling in the United States. But Oprah never picked up on that thread in a meaningful way. Instead, she resorted to platitudes: "We're doing this [program] so that every school will be as good as the best school. Because I believe, just as I know all of you watching believe, that every American child deserves the best school."

But if Oprah really thought her audience believed that, she could have gone further. She could have laid the funding and race questions on the table instead of allowing them to go unspoken. While she was at it, she could have pointed out that the hundreds of billions of dollars funneled into the military could go a long way toward achieving equity in our schools.

To her credit, Oprah did urge all parents—not just poor parents—to push for change in the system. "You need to elect people who are really going to get the job done for you and your children's future," she said. What she didn't say, but I'm sure she realizes, is that many in her upper-income suburban fan base already do just that: They elect lawmakers who "get the job done" by keeping things exactly as they are.

The Best (White, Middle-Class) Schools in Chicago

I rarely read *Chicago* magazine, but the October 2006 cover story caught my eye: "The Best Elementary Schools: 140 Winners in the City and Suburbs and What Makes Them Good."[3] Published by a *Tribune* subsidiary, *Chicago* targets an upscale audience. Its pages are flush with full-page advertisements for Graff Diamonds, Cadillacs, and Ritz-Carlton Residences. Flipping through the pages, I wondered how many of the magazine's subscribers or writers sent their kids to Chicago Public Schools (CPS). Still, I read on.

The article's authors explained that they "tunneled into a mountain of data" (all, it turns out, from one source: the Illinois State Board of Education [ISBE]) to unearth "all-around top performers" among schools in Chicagoland. While they claimed that evaluating schools based solely on numbers is "too reductionist," that's exactly what they did. Their chart listing Chicago's thirty "best" public elementary schools compares them in six areas: average class size, student-teacher ratio, teachers' average years of experience, teachers' average salary, per-student spending, and the percentage of students who meet or exceed state standards in core subjects.

I was bothered by both the criteria and the methodology, but what struck me most was how few of the schools on the list I recognized. That might not seem strange—after all, Chicago has 481 elementary schools. But in my work with student teachers over the years, I've visited dozens of elementary buildings, probably close to a hundred, mostly on the city's south and west sides. Of the 30 on *Chicago*'s list, I'd been in three.

My curiosity piqued, I went home and plugged the names of the schools into the ISBE database. I was hunting for numbers missing from the magazine's chart: data on the racial and socioeconomic composition of each school's student body. System-wide, as in many big-city districts, the overwhelming majority of students (85.6%) come from low-income households. Combined, African Americans (48.6%) and Latinos (37.6%) make up over 86% of the student population. Asians are 3.2% of the total, and just 8.1% of the system's students are White.

I didn't expect the demographics of the schools on *Chicago*'s list to reflect the system's demographics precisely. Even so, I was taken aback by what I found. In only seven of the magazine's 30 "best" schools are African American students the predominant racial group. Latinos are the largest group in two, and Asians in one. In 20 of the 30 schools, White students are the predominant racial group, and in seven of those, Whites make up 68% or more of the student body—even though just 8% of all students in CPS are White.

More glaring, in only five of the 30 "best" schools do even a majority of the students qualify as low-income. And in only one of those does the percentage (79%) come close to the system average of 86%. What's more, in nine of the 30 schools, the percentage of students from low-income families is less than 20%. Talk about apartheid education.

The only references to class in *Chicago*'s 12-page lead article, however, are either throwaway sentences or attempts to talk around the subject. Race isn't mentioned once. The single veiled reference comes when the authors ponder the "extra layers of worldly education" students at one Chicago school receive "by growing up in an urban mix." Yet even that seemingly harmless euphemism obscures more than it reveals: many of the city's neighborhoods continue to be segregated along race and class lines, and over half of CPS schools are racially isolated (more than 90% Black or 90% Latino).

Five years later, in 2011, *Chicago* showed that it hadn't learned from its mistakes. In its January issue, the magazine's editors chose to feature Chicago schools once again. This time, the spotlight was on the revival of Nettelhorst Elementary, "a failing educational backwater" that made an astounding turnaround "when some determined moms got involved."[4] The story focused on the many snazzy additions the moms helped bring to the school: a $130,000 Nate Berkus-designed kitchen, a "French-bistro-inspired cafeteria," a surround-sound system, an air-conditioned gym, a new science lab. And it trumpeted the school's jump in test scores. In 2001, only 35% of Nettelhorst students met or exceeded state standards, and by 2010, that number had risen to 86%.

Yet the article gave short shrift to another element of the school's extreme makeover (and neglected to cite specific figures): In 2001, 77% of Nettelhorst's students were low-income. Nine years later, only 31% of its kids were from poor families. In fact, the school's percentage of low-income students had decreased every year since the "turnaround" began. But to focus on that would be a buzzkill for *Chicago*'s readers.

The Stories We Tell

In *A People's History of the United States*, Howard Zinn outlines several ways historians can distort the past.[5] They can lie outright, they can omit details, or they can state the facts quickly and then "bury them in a mass of other information," signaling the reader that said facts, however disturbing, aren't very important in the grand scheme of things.

Such distortions aren't limited to stories we tell about the past, however. Like historians, journalists and television producers make choices: what to show and what to leave out, what's said and what goes unspoken, what to emphasize and what to minimize. These choices are unavoidable, of course—no historical or journalistic account tells a story completely. But once made, they say something about the storyteller's assumptions, beliefs, and worldview.

In the *Tribune's* commentary following the series on NCLB, the editorial board's conservative politics were laid bare. As for *The Oprah Winfrey Show* and *Chicago*, their editorial choices seem to be dictated more by a profit-driven desire to appease mainstream sensibilities. Even if we concede that Oprah and her producers hoped to "do good" by devoting an entire segment to inequities in public education, they clearly made calculations in determining how far to go. By dodging complexities they knew could implicate and possibly alienate their core audience, they ended up further mystifying the issues. And they allowed their viewers to remain, if they wished, in a bubble of isolation and absolution, where the challenges faced by city schools are somebody else's problem.

Those of us who believe differently need to continue to pay close attention to the silences in popular accounts of urban education, and to seek out public spaces where we can tell counter-narratives of our own: op-ed pages, letters to the editor, blogs, online discussion boards, community or city council meetings. There's not just an elephant in the room—there's a herd. As often as we can and as conspicuously as possible, we need to wave our arms, point each one out, and call it by name.

Chapter 13

Another Path
Is Possible

It's mid-March—testing week in Chicago—and for many administrators in the city's schools that means a laser-like, 24/7 focus on one thing: the ISAT, or Illinois Standards Achievement Test. But Amy Rome, the 3rd-year principal at NTA, an elementary school on the near South Side, has spent the past 15 minutes in a hallway brainstorming session with a representative from a neighborhood social service agency. The mother of several NTA students has been evicted from her apartment in a nearby public housing development—her unit boarded up while she was away—and the social service worker has come seeking Amy's help in finding temporary housing for the woman and her children.

As Amy sees it, this is an integral part of her job. Ask her about her school's vision—even during ISAT week—and you won't hear references to test scores or mantra-like chants of the latest educational jargon. "At NTA we're about knowing our kids and our families," she says. "We're about relationship-building, student support, and collaborative problem-solving with the community. We believe the community's challenges are the school's challenges."

Yet while she laments the obsession with high-stakes accountability that has beset the city's schools over the past decade or so, she also believes that her students' scores matter. "Using a single test score as the basis for assessing our kids is unfair," she tells me later. "It puts them at a disadvantage, and we don't like that. But at the same time, it's the reality of how students are being evaluated right now, so we have to be responsive to it. We absolutely don't teach to the tests, but it's cheating a child to dismiss the idea that they need to do well on them. We try to view testing as a way to navigate better opportunities for our students. It matters to us because it impacts their future."

But rather than allowing the crush of NCLB-related demands to dictate their direction, Amy and her staff have worked hard to see through the thicket and clear a different path. They've focused not only on a more demanding curriculum that encourages critical thinking, but on broad-based supports for students and families and on making NTA "a place where kids want to be."

Early Struggles

The school's full name is rarely heard these days, but when NTA opened to much fanfare in 2002, it was known as the National Teachers Academy. Nearly all of its students were African American and came from two nearby public housing developments. At the time, the central office's plan was to create a national model of professional development: a neighborhood school where a staff of "master teachers" guided a corps of student interns—while observers looked on via giant two-way mirrors. NTA's striking $47 million structure included a four-story classroom building and a connected community center with a swimming pool and gymnasium.

But from the beginning, NTA struggled. When Amy arrived in 2004 to serve as a liaison for the University of Illinois at Chicago, which had been asked by the district to help jump-start the school, NTA was already on its second principal. Tardiness was high and attendance was spotty. Teachers were reluctantly implementing a scripted reading program. Few extracurricular opportunities were available for students. Parent involvement was minimal. Test scores were among the worst in the city. And morale, in general, was sinking.

As UIC's liaison, Amy worked with the school's new administration and university faculty to target specific challenges. Little by little, she began to see progress. Her first project was to tackle the school's excessive tardiness problem, and after a semester of talking with parents, distributing alarm clocks to families who needed them, and pairing younger children with older ones who could help them cross busy streets on their way to school, tardiness shrunk from 10% to 15% each day to less than 3%.

But numerous challenges lingered, and the environment among staff at the school remained tense. Before the end of the year the new principal left, and her replacement didn't last much longer. In 2006, Amy was chosen as the school's fourth principal in five years.

Connecting with Parents

As a classroom teacher in Chicago for nearly a decade, Amy had long believed that building strong relationships with parents and community members was crucial. As principal, one of her first priorities was to make parents feel welcome at NTA and to provide them with opportunities for meaningful involvement. She reinvigorated a "parent room" that had gone largely unutilized, equipping it with a computer, phone, photocopier, and information on job training and GED classes. She met with parents every Friday morning to discuss their concerns and solicit their counsel. And she encouraged teachers to do all they could to communicate their desire to have parents and caregivers visit their classrooms.

"The building started to feel more like a community school," Amy says. "It gave us more opportunities to better understand the community, and it gave parents more opportunities to understand what we were trying to do with the kids. They really got in the mix of how the school works and started advising us. So now they call to let me know when something important is happening in the community, or come by to give feedback on what we're doing in the school, or just to help us keep an eye on safety."

Other initiatives built on these connections. The entire staff went on neighborhood walks before school began each year to connect with residents and reinforce the importance of students being present on the first day. A full-fledged in-school health clinic, initiated through the UIC partnership, opened to address the many unmet medical needs in the community. Teachers voted to scrap the canned reading program in favor of a balanced literacy approach that they developed themselves. Amy also targeted new hires and new partnerships that brought additional programming and resources: an art therapy program, an adolescent nurse psychologist, a drumming group, and a hip hop yoga class.

"The most important thing was building a team," she says. "The quality of a teacher in the classroom is what makes it or breaks it for kids. And we have some amazing teachers."

A Climate Where Learning
Becomes Possible

Walk around NTA these days and you're struck by all the good things that are happening. Outside a pre-kindergarten classroom, photographs of "guest readers" include several moms, a dad, an auntie, and an older sister. Inside, kids brainstorm ideas for how to pick up and move a heavy dresser.

"Pour some of the stuff out," says Marcus.

"Use a string," says Omani.

"I'd get my big brother to help," adds someone else.

"Excuse me," a little boy with tight braids says. "We could all carry it together!"

"Yeah!" several voices call in unison, agreeing that it's a brilliant idea. The teacher, Connie, calls four students to the front of the class and, in what seems like an act of magic, they lift the dresser that none of them alone could budge. The rest of the class applauds and then settles down to listen to a read-aloud of *Carrying,* a book about how people in various places around the world carry different things.

Upstairs in the music room, 4th-graders beat out call-and-response drum rhythms. It's a wonderful, open space—"The energy is good," says Holly, the teacher—with oversized windows lining the entire north side and the words *dream, believe, explore,* and *unite* splashed on other walls. There's a circle of 22 painted drums, four congas, and, on a raised platform, xylophones, metalaphones, and a glockenspiel.

"Oh, that's so gorgeous," Holly says to the kids as they beat out a pattern in unison. Because they have spent most of the morning glued to their desks filling in test bubbles, Holly knows that music class may be a time for them to release frustrations. "I understand you had a really tough, stressful morning," she tells them. "But we still have to make good choices."

With every beat on the drums and every mallet-strike on the xylophones, I can almost see the tension being lifted from the kids' shoulders. One student, Raymond, goes a little overboard with his drumming technique and is asked to sit out for awhile, but for the most part, the next 45 minutes are full of movement, singing, and syncopated rhythms—kids being given the time and space to connect with their creative spirits. It shouldn't feel like such a novelty, but on the South Side of Chicago, in the middle of a school day, it does.

Later in a physical education class, the teacher, Aaron, begins by having his 8th-graders put on pedometers. They discuss whether the gadgets measure the volume or intensity of exercise, then huddle up to play a team-building game.

At the end of the period, Aaron has all the students check their pedometers to see how many steps they took during the 50-minute class. The kids then sit in a circle and Aaron asks them to hold up between one and five fingers, giving themselves two grades: one for effort and one for attitude. He asks if anybody wants to nominate a classmate for a sportsmanship award, and hands shoot up. "I nominate Kiara," one boy says, "because she got frustrated but she didn't quit." Several other kids follow by nominating another of their peers.

When I ask Aaron how he developed such a supportive atmosphere among these teenagers, he says it's mostly due to the trusting relationships he's built with them—not just in the classroom, but also coaching and working with them after school. "I think sometimes kids need to be helped to find the language to say nice things to each other," he says. "I want them to feel safe here, and I want them to feel cared for. That's when learning can happen. We're trying to create a climate here where learning becomes possible."

It's a philosophy Amy has actively promoted and the entire school has embraced: Creating a climate where real learning becomes possible. And it's not a coincidence that when you ask Amy to let you visit a few classrooms, she includes the music and P.E. classes. At some schools, these have become afterthoughts, little more than once-weekly diversions in the quest for higher test scores and AYP. But Amy believes that the drumming and the teambuilding exercises and the parent center and the yoga classes have done just as much to create a climate for learning as have the balanced literacy program and the renewed focus on academic rigor.

"It's so great to see the kids learning," she says. "To see them motivated, to see them feeling good about themselves, to see them believing that it's cool to be academically smart."

Telpochcalli: Culture at the Center

A few miles away, on the southwest side of the city, Telpochcalli, a small public elementary school that serves 260 mostly Mexican immigrant students, has been doing things differently for 15 years. Telpochcalli, which means "house of youth," was founded in 1994 by a group of teachers, including current principal Tamara Witzl, as a K-8 school that would center its curriculum on the culture, language, and artistic traditions of its students.

"We made a commitment to do things differently here from the beginning," Tamara says. "And we hold each other to that commitment." The school's approach is constructed on four pillars: building a strong professional learning community, working in genuine partnership with the surrounding community, educating students to be fully bilingual and biliterate, and infusing Mexican art and culture into all subject areas. All of these come together, Tamara says, to create an environment that keeps social justice at the center of the school's mission.

Educating Against the Grain

Telpochcalli's approach goes against the grain of current educational policy in almost every way. The past decade has seen relentless attacks against bilingual education nationally, and in Chicago the push has been toward moving students out of bilingual classrooms and into English-only classes as quickly as possible. Tamara sees a strong correlation between these developments and the increased focus on standardized test scores. But she says Telpochcalli is committed to bilingualism for the long term. "We believe it's a good thing for all students. We want our kids to value and hold on to their home language and to learn English as well, to be truly bilingual and biliterate."

One of the most tragic casualties of the preoccupation with testing in many urban schools has been the arts. At Telpochcalli, Tamara not only seeks out grants to fund artists-in-residence and after-school programs in guitar, video production, and folkloric dancing, but she also actively promotes the infusion of the arts in every subject area during the school day. The hallways and classrooms are alive with creativity—vibrant floor-to-ceiling murals, colorful student paintings and pottery, marimbas, video cameras, the sounds of Mexican *corridos* or *rancheras* spilling out of an open classroom door.

Like Amy, Tamara keeps an eye on test scores, but she refuses to let such concerns overwhelm the broader vision of Telpochcalli. "We believe in the popular education model," she says. "Building capacity and using education as a means of doing that." It makes sense, then, that the school is a true community center, offering ESL classes for adults, aerobics and sewing courses, men's basketball nights, domestic violence workshops, and a lot more. In a given week more than 400 people use the building outside of school hours.

"We want to be open and available to kids and families," Tamara explains. "We're continually stretching ourselves, and we're committed to meeting people's needs when they come to us and how they come to us. You have to make very overt, constant efforts to keep the doors open and keep working with people."

That work doesn't end at the schoolhouse door, however. In 1998, Tamara joined a group of neighborhood parents, educators, and activists in founding a nonprofit organization, the Telpochcalli Community Education Project, which operates both inside and outside schools in efforts "to bring about a more united, better educated, safer, and socially prepared community."

It isn't just the work Tamara and her staff do that is nontraditional. The way they work is unconventional as well. Rather than the top-down administrative model—resurgent, perhaps, because of so many federal and district mandates—Telpochcalli is about shared leadership and consensus building. To help make that possible, the school's teachers decided early on that they needed more opportunities to come together to share ideas, develop curriculum, and grow professionally. So they agreed to restructure the day—scheduling longer teaching days Monday through Thursday—so that every Friday afternoon would be dedicated to whole-staff gatherings and professional development.

Schools as They Could Be

As principal, Tamara sees her role largely as helping to facilitate the shared vision. While her days are partly filled with the kinds of tasks one might expect of a school administrator—answering calls and emails, helping to monitor hallways and lunchrooms, completing district-required paperwork—she believes her most valuable contribution lies in supporting others in their work. "I try to help people solve problems and stay connected with one another," she says. "I help seek out resources and supports. And a major part of what I do is remaining firmly committed to our work and our way of working—so that we don't roll back into the same old, same old."

Tamara acknowledges that being part of a small school has made it easier in some respects to resist the "same old, same old" and navigate the pressures of NCLB. She calls herself a "hard-core small schools person," and believes that the nature of larger buildings with hundreds more students can lead principals to fall back, sometimes unintentionally, on traditional forms of leadership. She also thinks the "enormous fear factor" of not making AYP may inhibit some administrators from thinking more creatively. "But our approach is, if it's an idea that is supportive of what we're trying to do, then we try to find a way to make it work."

Of course, it's hard to blame principals for being fearful. The entire framework of No Child Left Behind has revolved around threats and punishment for schools that don't "perform" since its inception. Superintendents or school CEOs often pass that fear on to their subordinates, who pass it on to principals, who pass it on to teachers, who pass it on to students. But Tamara and the teachers at Telpochcalli serve as a reminder that it doesn't have to be that way, that it's possible, even under the cloud of NCLB, to hold on to a vision of schools as they could be.

Visionary Leadership

Yet the cloud still hovers overhead. While NTA's reading and math scores have risen dramatically in the past 3 years, the school still doesn't meet NCLB's Adequate Yearly Progress goals. And though Telpochcalli meets AYP in all other categories, it continues to miss the mark in reading.

For Tamara, this says far less about what's happening at the schools than it does about the inherent limits of No Child Left Behind's measures—as well as the law's disregard for the influence of outside-school factors such as poverty and substandard health care on students' performance in school. "There are some really good reasons the data looks the way it does," she says. "If we're really serious about leveling the opportunities, we need to get serious at the policy level about having wrap-around support systems for kids and families."

In the meantime, mandates and dictums rain down on principals on a seemingly daily basis, and how they respond—determining which to attend to seriously, which to send straight to the recycle bin, and which fall somewhere in-between—can make a huge difference in what sort of learning environment is promoted and nurtured at a school. It's a team effort, of course, and Amy and Tamara are both quick to acknowledge the crucial efforts of their teachers, staff, parent volunteers, and other partners. When discussing their schools' approaches, they talk about "we" far more than "I." Still, it would be hard to overstate the importance of courageous, visionary, imaginative leadership—especially in times like these.

Amy and Tamara agree that it's difficult work, but also deeply satisfying. "What we do at Telpochcalli requires flexibility and stability and a commitment to doing it day after day after day," Tamara says. "It's not easy to sustain. But I wouldn't want to do it any other way."

Amy adds: "When you think about the scope of the job, there are so many things you have to do that it can be pretty overwhelming. It can be hard to focus on the things that really matter. But despite the craziness, we're inspired by the commitment everybody in the school makes—especially the kids. The hope and the possibility you see in the kids keeps you coming back every day."

Chapter 14

The Trouble with "Innovation" in Schools

I was sitting among a large crowd of students and teachers at the Chicago Public Schools Video Fair. It was 1998—four years before No Child Left Behind was signed into law, but already 3 years into Chicago's own march toward test-driven "accountability."

I listened as a high-level district administrator stepped to the podium to congratulate a group of my 7th-graders on winning the festival's top prize. Their video, which they'd made in my media studies class, was a portrayal of how racist attitudes are passed on from adults to children.

I don't recall all of the administrator's words, but I remember her commending the students, recognizing our school's media studies program, and ending with, "I'm sure participating in this program is really raising the students' reading scores!"

Applause followed, but I left feeling deflated. I believed the media studies course was beneficial for many of our school's 7th- and 8th-graders. At its best, it gave them space to voice their opinions on issues, to become more critical consumers of media messages, and, broadly speaking, to become more literate. Maybe even more importantly, it provided an outlet for the kids to express themselves creatively.

But none of that seemed to matter much when held up against the new priorities. It became clear to me that afternoon that we'd taken a few more steps down a perilous, narrow path in Chicago. We'd reached a place where the value of any classroom project or school program would ultimately be judged by whether it boosted reading or math scores on the yearly standardized tests.

Flash forward 13 years and many miles down that same path. Both the media studies class at my former school and the CPS Video Fair are long gone and buried. Their demise reflects what many of the teachers in my current graduate classes—especially those in city schools that serve poor students—describe as their daily reality: more top-down control of what is taught (and at what pace), less support for teacher and student creativity, less time for the arts and other non-tested subjects, and a laser-like focus on moving scores higher.

An irony in all this is that one of the favored words of the business-minded reformers who continue to push a results-driven, corporate model of school change is "innovation." Of all the buzzwords that zip through current conversations about school improvement, it may be the most repeated. It peppers the language of Race to the Top, of charter school cheerleading, of teacher recruitment pitches—if you're not talking about innovating, you're probably not getting heard.

But the word, like so many others in education, has been hijacked. The "new reformers" have appropriated it as a descriptor for policy proposals and practices they advocate, and as an antonym for almost anything else. Charter schools? Innovative. Regular public schools? Definitely not. Competing for education funding? Innovative. Assuring that adequate monies go to schools that most need them? Old school.

Corporate reformers have come to own the word so completely that they're able to promote even the most wrongheaded ideas and still be portrayed by many media outlets as innovators. Bill Gates proclaimed that we should crowd more students into the classrooms of the "top 25% of teachers" in order to save money.[1] Does any school-based educator believe that that's a good idea? The film *Waiting for Superman*,[2] a favorite of the innovation crowd, put forth an image of student learning that is as ill-conceived as it is crude: the empty-vessel head of a cartoon student is opened up and a pile of information is poured in. It's all about efficiency—more head-filling, less fact-spilling. But hey, that's innovation!

Because many of the practices, values, and jargon ("Are you tracking me?") of the new reformers have been borrowed from the business world, it's also important to remember that what corporate CEOs celebrate as innovative isn't necessarily fair or just. Bob Herbert's final column[3] for the *New York Times* lamented the growing wealth gap in the United States, and highlighted the fact that General Electric, which racked up $14.2 billion in profits in 2010, paid zero federal taxes. With so many families struggling to make ends meet, how can this be? According to the *Times*'s own reporting,

G.E. implements "an aggressive strategy that mixes fierce lobbying for tax breaks and *innovative accounting* (italics mine) that enables it to concentrate its profits offshore."[4]

I'm all for fresh ideas, but just because a notion is novel or different doesn't mean it's good for teachers and kids. The trouble with many of the current "innovations" in education is that they do nothing to challenge a broader policy framework that prizes higher test scores above all else—in fact, they often embrace it. So teacher and student creativity will continue to be squashed at every turn. And the poorer the kids in the classroom or school, the more likely that is to be true.

That, for me, is the most troubling aspect of where we appear to be headed. States and schools have been permitted to escape the pressure cooker of AYP-chasing that has marked the past decade, and that's a good thing. But the test-driven focus remains. And for the 5% of schools at the bottom of the test-score pile—mostly schools of the urban poor—the heat will be turned up even higher: more testing, more "data-driven" instruction, and more sanctions, while creativity, divergent thinking, and the arts continue to get left behind.

I think about the 7th- and 8th-graders I taught in Chicago—kids like Ramon, who daydreamed in poetic verse but had a hard time sitting still, or Josefina, a recent immigrant who struggled with English but found her voice when a video camera was in her hands. What place is there for kids like them in the schools we've made? How will they discover their gifts, pursue their dreams? And if they become alienated by their schooling experiences—which seems likely—where will they turn?

It depends on who you ask, I suppose. Michelle Rhee, former DC schools chancellor and one of the rock-star "innovators" in education, famously told *Time* magazine in 2008:

> The thing that kills me about education is that it's so touchy-feely. People say, "Well, you know, test scores don't take into account creativity and the love of learning." I'm like, "You know what? I don't give a crap." Don't get me wrong. Creativity is good and whatever. But if the children don't know how to read, I don't care how creative you are. You're not doing your job.[5]

On the other hand, Sir Ken Robinson, Professor Emeritus at the University of Warwick and author of *Out of Our Minds*, argues in a widely

circulated talk from the TED conference[6] that schools too often end up
stifling kids' creative spirits. "Creativity is as important in education as literacy," Robinson says, "and we should treat it with the same status."

We should—but with the continued reliance on annual testing in federal policy, it may not happen anytime soon. That means too many kids
in our poorest neighborhoods will continue to receive what can only be
called an impoverished education—even if their test scores rise. And no
matter what the new reformers say, there's nothing innovative about that.

Chapter 15

Race to the Top of What?

In Search of the
Democratic Ideal in Education

In Chicago, the mayor pressures public school teachers to accept a 25% longer school day for a 2% increase in pay—while his own children attend an exclusive private school.

In Texas, a conservative state board of education approves revised social studies standards that emphasize the "superiority of American capitalism"[1] while minimizing the historical contributions of Latinos.

In Florida, legislators pass a statewide merit pay program that will hand out cash bonuses of up to $25,000 to teachers who raise student test scores.

In Brooklyn, a former teacher at a lauded charter school recalls a typical day: students with "hands folded in front of them, backs firmly against the back of their seats, and eyes on the teacher at all times . . . while we forced endless test prep down their throats."[2]

To proponents of market-based approaches to school reform, this is what democracy looks like: competition, standardization, efficiency, and—to carry it all out on a daily basis—a cadre of compliant teachers. The lexicon of the new reformers comes straight from the business world, and their strategies for improving schools owe more to Rupert Murdoch than John Dewey. Their basic assumptions have been repeated in the mainstream media so often that they are accepted by many as conventional wisdom: Public schools are failing. U.S. students are falling far behind those in other countries. Too many teachers are inept and need to be fired. The only way to truly measure learning is with standardized tests.

As Linda Darling-Hammond[3] has pointed out, this corporate model of school reform is not without precedent. In the early 1900s, a previous wave of "scientific managers" sought to accomplish similar ends in schools. But Franklin Bobbitt and his followers never swept into the national consciousness—or the halls of government—like the disciples of the Bill Gates/Eli Broad School of Education have.[4] And at least education was Bobbitt's lifelong field of expertise. In the current debate over the direction of American schools, there's only one surefire way to be heard: Don't be an educator.

The principles of democracy and the machinations of the market have long been at odds in U.S. society. No matter what 8th-grade textbooks say, the two simply can't coexist comfortably, and never have. The same Founders who put a stake in the ground for liberty and equality were also quick to divvy up that ground and claim ownership of it. Then as now, the contradictions were stark. These days, with the notable recent exception of the Occupy movement, the lore of capitalism—the wisdom of the market, the gospel of wealth, the primacy of self-interest—is increasingly passed off as "the American story," while the democratic ideal shrinks in the background. We esteem free markets, it often seems, far more than free minds or free people.

In their book *Expect Miracles*, Peter Cookson and Kristina Berger write that two grand narratives—two opposing visions—compete for attention in America: the narrative of greatness, and the narrative of goodness.[5] The narrative of America the Great is based on manifest destiny, dominance, accumulation, and more than a bit of hubris. On the other hand, the narrative of goodness is based on community, democratic values, a diversity of voices, and a dedication to justice and equality. "If we pursue the narrative of greatness," the authors write, "our children will become economic and military warriors, blinded by pride of victory and the struggle for dominance."[6] If, on the other hand, we teach the goodness narrative, they will work toward a compassionate, humane, and just society.

Looking at what's happened in schools over the past decade, it seems clear that the narrative of greatness is the one we are pursuing. We spend most of our time focused on high test scores and narrowly defined achievement—the things we've convinced ourselves are most essential if we are to compete, and dominate, in the global marketplace. Rather than questioning the workings of that marketplace—asking who it serves and who it crushes, asking what the alternatives might be—we instead keep both eyes fixed on "greatness." What should trouble us, though, is that in the pursuit of "great" schools, we're losing sight of what makes good schools. We're losing sight of the gap between what we believe, deep down, education in a democracy should be, and what we have all been complicit in allowing it to become.

* * *

It's tempting to lay all the blame for this on No Child Left Behind, Race to the Top, and the simultaneous torrid takeover by the corporate-style reform movement. But even before this wave of repressive changes, too few schools took seriously their responsibility as caretakers of the democratic project. Thinking back on my years as a teacher in Chicago, I can't remember one faculty meeting, professional development session, or school district gathering where the word *democracy* or *democratic* was even uttered. While my colleagues and I took for granted that we taught and lived *in* a democracy, we too rarely had conversations about how best to live *out* the democratic ideal within our classrooms and beyond.

Still, the policies of the last ten years haven't helped. Yes, some of the people who supported NCLB at the beginning had good intentions. And as Mike Rose[7] has noted, the law certainly has democratic impulses: paying specific attention to groups of children who have been historically ill-served by schools, highlighting the need for quality teachers in all schools (not just those that serve the privileged), renewing the notion that public institutions should be responsible to the people. If nothing else, at least the imagery of NCLB nodded in the direction we need to be headed. If the choice is between leaving no child behind and racing to the top, I'll take the former any day. As Stanley Fish commented in the *New York Times*, "Race to the top of what?"[8]

One of the main reasons No Child Left Behind put educators in such a bind is that it failed to recognize a basic truth: Schools do not exist in a vacuum. If stark inequities exist outside the schoolhouse doors, they will manifest themselves inside classrooms as well. Yet while federal policies demand that schools make "adequate yearly progress" on closing the test score gap, no such expectations exist for remedying the harsh conditions that impact kids' lives outside schools. Veteran teacher Stan Karp[9] points out that test-score differences largely reflect social disparities that disproportionately impact African Americans and Latinos: levels of family income, school funding, unemployment, incarceration, wealth. "Why are there no federal mandates demanding the elimination of these gaps?" Karp asks. "Don't these inequalities leave children behind?"

Not according to many of the new reformers. In their world, outside-school factors such as poverty, food insecurity, and even racism are merely "excuses"—and excuses aren't permitted to get in the way of achievement on standardized tests. Even President Obama jumped on the no excuses bandwagon in a 2009 speech to the NAACP. After acknowledging that Black children continue to face additional challenges, especially if they are poor, he added, "but that's not a reason to give up on your education and drop out of school . . . No excuses. No excuses."[10] On *The Colbert Report* the night after the speech, Stephen Colbert wondered, with tongue in cheek, if lead poisoning counted as an excuse.

Many people, myself included, were hopeful that Obama's election would bring a new direction to educational policy on the federal level. But in his first three years in office, Obama and his education secretary, former Chicago schools' CEO Arne Duncan, offered little change. Education historian Diane Ravitch famously remarked that Obama had given George Bush a third term in office on education policy.[11] Under Obama's and Duncan's leadership, we headed further down the same road we traveled the previous eight years: more testing, more school closings, more charter schools, more corporate style reform. And in some respects, things got even worse: efforts to marginalize teachers' unions; threats to fire teachers en masse; and merit pay schemes that seemed destined to promote competition, rather than collaboration, among colleagues.

Many classroom teachers I've worked with over the last decade questioned the direction of the new reforms. Even teachers whose students' test scores increased sometimes wondered if it was worth all they were sacrificing in the process. A few weeks before the end of school in 2011, I sent out an e-mail asking teachers I know to write about "what mattered" to them that year. Jenna, a 3rd-grade teacher I'd taught when she was an undergraduate, described her mixed feelings this way:

> We received our [test] scores last Friday. Twenty-one of my 26 students passed. Chicago Public Schools and the administration would say that mattered. However, I honestly cannot agree. Although I breathed a huge sigh of relief

when I saw the results, I still feel like I cheated my students out of a year. They passed a test that allows them to continue on to 4th grade, but I don't feel that they learned anything from that. From January to March all we taught was [test] prep. It was torture for me and for my students. I'm sure there are some other things that mattered this year to my students, but because of the huge emphasis on the tests, most of my students would say passing the [test] was what mattered. In my short five years in Chicago, education has gone down-hill, and unfortunately what I think matters cannot even be taught.[12]

Even the much-celebrated test score gains, when examined more close-ly, are often minimal, if not imaginary. Besides the high-profile cheating scandals in Atlanta, Philadelphia, and other cities, mounting research evidence suggests that the education policies of the Bush and Obama years have been ineffective even at their own narrow aims.

In Chicago, a succession of schools' CEOs since the mid-1990s has boasted of impressive yearly bumps in student scores systemwide. But in a 2011 report[13] that synthesized 20 years of research on school reform in the city, the Consortium on Chicago School Research found that statistics used by the district for year-to-year test score comparisons were seriously flawed. When properly adjusted, reading scores in Chicago elementary schools showed almost no growth over the 20-year period. Even worse, the gap in reading scores between White and African American students actually *increased* over the past two decades.

Of course, these findings run counter to the narrative central office administrators have woven over the years. But they don't come as a sur-prise to Chicagoans who've read between the lines of district press releases. Even a cursory look at the list of schools that score highest on annual tests reveals glaring disparities mapped onto race and class differences. At the 15 Chicago elementary schools with the highest test scores in 2010, only 19% of students, on average, were low-income. Contrast that to the district as a whole, where 86% of students are poor, and we might as well be at Hogwarts using the Sorting Hat. As Pauline Lipman[14] has noted, it's a dual system, still separate and unequal.

The larger point, though, is this: The obsession with market-driven reforms in public schools is more than just ineffective; it's undemocratic. No Child Left Behind's restrictive mandates eroded community control of schools, diminished teacher voice, and—in too many cases—all but extinguished a broad-based, humanistic approach to curriculum. Race to the Top's very name promised a capitalist, rather than democratic, vision, and made good on that pledge by engineering a funding competition that could only be won by states that embraced the "right" reforms. Most damning of all, the focus on high-stakes testing—an essential component of all the market-driven strategies—actually plays out at ground level as a monumental distraction. It encourages school-based educators to spend all their time focusing on compliance, appearances, and "data" rather than on more essential questions that have gotten lost in the high-stakes shuffle: Education toward what end? What, after all, are the purposes of public schools in a democracy?

* * *

Next time you're at the grocery store, stop a random person and ask what the purpose of schools in America should be. Along with a few crazy looks, you're likely to get a range of answers: To prepare young people for the work force. To teach the basics. To keep kids off the streets. But suggest to your interviewee that one of the primary purposes should be to prepare students to be engaged, thoughtful citizens—participants, not spectators, in the lives of their communities—and she would probably nod in agreement. That statement, no matter where it might be uttered in this country, probably wouldn't spark much debate. But it raises another question, a thornier one, which Joel Westheimer and Joe Kahne[15] phrase this way: What *kind* of citizen do we need to support an effective democratic society?

Westheimer and Kahne spent two years studying school-based programs in the United States that aim to promote democracy. They discovered that such programs offer vastly different ideas about what it means to be a good citizen. The conception that is most common in school programs is what they call the "personally responsible citizen."[16] This view of citizenship is often promoted by character education programs, and emphasizes honesty, respect, obeying rules, loyalty, and volunteerism. In many schools, parents and teachers would no doubt applaud such goals. But Westheimer and Kahne suggest that this approach is not only "an inadequate response to the challenges of educating a democratic citizenry"[17]—but that it can actually work in opposition to truly democratic aims.

That's because the spotlight on individual responsibility may send students the message that personal acts of charity are all that are needed to redress injustices. That, in turn, may dissuade them from examining the causes of social ills. In addition, the emphasis on loyalty and obedience can encourage passivity rather than activism, complacency rather than critical civic engagement. While many of the individual characteristics emphasized by personally responsible citizenship may be laudable, Westheimer and Kahne observe, that doesn't mean they equate with creating democratic citizens.[18]

If we want to prepare kids to be thoughtful and engaged participants in a democracy, the authors say, we need to promote what they term a "justice-oriented"[19] conception of citizenship. That means an emphasis not just on civic participation, but further, on a critical analysis of the root causes of social inequalities and a commitment to take action to address them. It means an acknowledgment that, in a democracy, individual behaviors and virtues, no matter how admirable, are not enough. Social change happens because of the collective efforts of citizens—from grassroots community organizing to broader social movements and public policy initiatives.

If we don't take seriously the task of preparing citizens, then in a very real sense the foundation of our democracy is in jeopardy. And we can't take it seriously if we continue to provide a qualitatively different education for children depending on their zip code. As the conveners of the Forum for Education and Democracy write, "The students most poorly served by the educational system go on to be adults with the least voice, involvement, and influence in their communities. With unequal education we set up a cycle where . . . today's underserved students will be tomorrow's disenfranchised citizens."[20]

That means we need schools in poor and immigrant communities that aren't test-prep factories. We need schools that value deep thinking and problem-solving over testing booklets, schools that promote discussion and debate rather than drill and kill, schools that foster community engagement, that encourage kids to think, to wonder, to speak up and speak out.

We also need schools that value and support teachers, schools where teachers' collective voices and ideas are the beating heart of daily practice. But in too many places, that's not the case. District-level administrators issue directives to principals, who pass them on to teachers, who are expected to obediently "carry them out" in the classroom. Many teachers I know, especially younger ones, feel disempowered and overwhelmed. Rather than seeing themselves as partners in a democratic enterprise, they feel like the interchangeable cogs of a mammoth, grinding machine. Rob, a third-year middle school teacher and a student in one of my graduate classes, said one night: "I totally get how schools can be oppressive places for kids. But right now I think teachers are oppressed, too. At least where I work they are. We have no voice. We have no say. None. We're told what to do and that's it. Whether we believe in it or not, whether we agree or not—it doesn't matter."

His response reminded me of an e-mail I received a few years prior from a woman I'd taught in a certification program for career changers. She'd become a teacher in Chicago with high hopes and seemingly boundless energy, determined to create a meaningful learning experience for her kids. I'd observed her in action several times, and found her to be a wonderful, gifted teacher.

"This is a difficult email for me," she wrote. "After months of weighing options and struggling with the complexity of it all, I have decided to resign from Chicago Public Schools. When I went into teaching, I was not naive to the challenges in CPS; I understood that the adventure I was embarking on would be tough. [But] I have really struggled this year to justify the focus on test scores, rather than student learning. . . . Trust me, this was not an easy decision. . . . but as the year went on, and the testing season approached, I realized how much of a mismatch my priorities are with the CPS administration. My personality will not allow me to just shut my door and teach."[21]

✳ ✳ ✳

For teachers and students, it's tough to live out democratic practice in schools where your own voice goes unheard, where decisions are made or policies are put in place in decidedly undemocratic ways. Having to deal with the crush of day-to-day demands and mandates—no matter how much individual teachers may dislike them or disagree with them—can make it difficult to keep an eye on the kinds of schools we might imagine. But our imaginations may well be our greatest allies. "Imagination," Maxine Greene has written, "alters the vision of the way things are; it opens spaces in experience where projects can be devised, the kinds of projects that may bring things closer to what ought to be."[22] Rekindling our collective imagination, reminding ourselves of what is possible, is one of the most crucial tasks for educators in this time of shifted priorities and narrowing visions. It's a testament to the resilience, spirit, and creativity of so many teachers that they manage to do so despite the data-driven whirlwind that spins around them.

Adam Heenan, a former student of mine who's now a high school social studies teacher on the southwest side, is a tireless education activist outside the classroom who strives to live out his ideals inside it. When Maya, a student in his Street Law class, was unhappy with her grade on an assignment, Adam told her to prepare a case to present to the class. A few days later, he and Maya took turns laying out their arguments to a tribunal made up of several of her classmates. Adam used the assignment rubric as evidence; Maya used her completed project. After hearing both sides, the tribunal had the final say on whether the student's grade should be changed, and they found in favor of their teacher. Maya was somewhat disappointed in the ruling, but told Adam the experience was empowering because she'd never had the opportunity to challenge a teacher's grade. "I think it's important for teens to understand that they can advocate for themselves," Adam says. "And to see that human beings and their laws and rules are fallible and need to be challenged."

In another Chicago school, student teacher Beto Sepúlveda used a printmaking lesson in his 6th- through 8th-grade art classes as a tie-in to the struggle for immigration reform. Beto guided his Mexican immigrant students in designing and printing posters, which they carried while marching in a large immigrant rights demonstration downtown. "We are all immigrants," one of the posters read. "*Venimos a trabajar—No somos criminales*," [We come to work—We are not criminals] said another. At the march, the kids videotaped interviews with other participants, then showed their footage at school a few days later. Parents and neighborhood residents were invited to attend the screening and to discuss next steps. For Beto and his students, what started as an art lesson turned into a powerful exercise in community-building and democratic practice.

Sometimes it's students who take the lead in opening up democratic spaces in schools. During the 2011 mayoral campaign in Chicago, three juniors from Sullivan High School were alarmed when they heard candidate

Rahm Emanuel, a fervent supporter of charter schools, say in a televised debate that all but two of the top-performing high schools in the city were charters.[23] The three students—Alexandra Alvarez, Gerardo Aguilera, and Cristina Henriquez—doubted Emanuel's claim and undertook some research of their own. Armed with their findings and a Flip camera, they put together a simple but powerful video and posted it on YouTube.

"Somebody didn't do their homework," the video declares after a clip of Emanuel's quote on charters from the debate. A list of the top seven best-scoring high schools in Chicago then scrolls up the screen, followed by the words, "None are charter schools." The YouTube video went viral in Chicago, and focused attention not only on Emanuel's egregious error on a key campaign issue, but on the importance of the voices of youth in the election.

Outside of my immediate circles in Chicago, I've long looked to the pages of the journal *Rethinking Schools* for examples of democratic practice. It's a publication full of incisive commentary and great ideas, and many of its articles are written by classroom teachers. In one issue, Bob Peterson, a 5th-grade teacher in Milwaukee and one of *Rethinking Schools'* founding editors, recounts a teachable moment that began with a lesson about the American Revolution.[24] During the lesson, Peterson explained to his class that George Washington owned 317 enslaved Africans. A student added that Thomas Jefferson was a slave owner as well. Then another student asked a question that nobody in the class could answer: "Which other presidents owned slaves?"

Peterson told his kids he had no idea which presidents had owned slaves. But instead of brushing the question off and pressing forward with his plans, he encouraged the students to search for answers. With Peterson's help, they tried looking in their textbook, a World Book Encyclopedia, an online encyclopedia, and the school library, but found nothing. So over the next few weeks, they did lots more digging—mostly online. What they eventually found after piecing together information from multiple sources was that ten of the first 18 U.S. presidents were slave owners.

But the project didn't end there. After discussing why this important knowledge was so hard to uncover, the students had another idea: write a letter to the publisher of their textbook to ask why the information hadn't been included. So they did. They also asked why the word *racism* wasn't included one time in the book's 700 pages. "Dear editors of United States Fifth Grade Textbook," one student wrote,

I am a fifth grader at La Escuela Fratney. I am 11 years old and I like to read and write. When I am reading I notice every little word . . . I see that you do not mention that some of the presidents had slaves. But some of them did. Like George Washington had 317 slaves. So did Thomas Jefferson. He had 267 slaves. If you want to teach children the truth, then you should write the truth. The children should really know the truth about the Presidents. Or do you know the truth about the Presidents?

To its credit, the publishing company had a representative write back to the class. But it wasn't the most convincing letter. Part of it read: "The first issue you wrote about concerns the absence of the word 'racism' in the text. While the word 'racism' does not appear, the subject of unfair treatment of people because of their race is addressed on page 467 when segregation is explained."

Peterson's project grew out of his students' questions and concerns. It engaged them in a collaborative quest for learning with a purpose. It allowed them to challenge the official textbook account of history, and gave them space to take action on what they'd learned. The democratic ideal breathed to life.

It's happening outside classrooms, too. Parents, grassroots groups, and community organizations are all crucial partners in a truly democratic educational project. In 2010 the Chicago Grassroots Curriculum Taskforce (CGCT), a group of local education activists, launched a multifaceted effort to "revolutionize the traditional educational model of classroom learning"[25] with original curriculum that connects to students' lives and experiences. CGCT opened a resource center that includes educational materials, children's books, DVDs, and primary source materials—all with a focus on local context, cultural relevance, and social justice. To build their library of locally created curriculum, they solicit lesson submissions from area teachers and students, and are co-creating an original unit for 3rd- to 12th-graders called *A People's Chicago: Our Stories of Change and Struggle.*

With the prevalence of standardized, top-down, decontextualized approaches to curriculum, CGCT's work is a reminder that the democratic ideal demands something far different. Curriculum should, as the conveners of the Forum for Education and Democracy put it, "actively engage students in exploring their world" and "delve deeply into the conflicting claims inherent in democracy itself."[26] This is not the sort of curriculum that's delivered by textbook companies in shiny boxes. Rather, like democracy itself, it is collaborative, a work in progress, built from the ground up.

Democratic practice in schools can also involve rethinking traditional partnerships. Illinois State University's Chicago Teacher Education Pipeline works closely with two community-based organizations, Enlace Chicago and the Greater Auburn-Gresham Community Development Corporation, to operate year-long Professional Development School programs. Groups of 20 to 30 ISU students spend their entire senior year in Chicago, participating in a demanding year-long teaching internship. Many also live in university-subsidized housing in the community where they're teaching.

While most PDSs nationwide are partnerships between a university and a school district, ISU's Pipeline sought to create three-way partnerships—with the third partner, the community-based organization, being a crucial added dimension. Student interns benefit from the community organization's deep knowledge of their neighborhood, and the students' intensive learning about local contexts gives them a deeper understanding of their students' lives. Ideally, it's an arrangement that acknowledges the reciprocal nature of a democratic education: that all who partake should be both teachers and learners. For many universities engaged in work in urban schools and communities, that has been an exceedingly difficult guideline to keep in mind.

Finally, while the dominant narrative of the moment is all about competing in the global marketplace—or "winning the future,"[27] to use President Obama's unfortunate phrase—some educators conceive of a globally aware education quite differently. The National Network for Educational Renewal, for example, advocates "creating citizens of the world"[28]—a phrase that conjures Martin Luther King Jr.'s "beloved community" rather than a macroeconomics version of the reality show *Survivor*. Instead of asking how we can best out-learn and out-earn "rival" countries, we might try reframing our questions: How can we understand one another better across borders or languages or cultures? How can we work together to be stewards of the planet? Instead of focusing only on what we can sell or outsource to others, how about asking what can we learn from them?

Some school districts and states don't seem interested in entertaining questions such as these. Instead, they're trimming bilingual education programs, outlawing ethnic studies courses, or passing English-only laws. But others are thinking differently—not only about the kind of schools they want to create, but the kind of world they want their children to inherit. And more importantly, how their children can be engaged and enlightened citizens in that world.

In San Francisco, the board of education passed a resolution to provide bilingual education to all students in the city by 2023, and enacted a robust multilingual learning plan. As of 2010, the city had language immersion programs in 21 schools, with students spending up to 90% of their classroom time in kindergarten and first grade learning a target language, and then gradually transitioning to more English instruction each year. The immersion programs include Mandarin, Cantonese, Spanish, and Korean, with French, Russian, and German options in the pipeline. This wouldn't be news in many other countries, where learning two or more languages in school is the norm. But in the United States, where we have clung firmly to an English-only worldview, San Francisco's schools are well ahead of the curve.

The documentary film *Speaking in Tongues*[29] follows a year in the lives of several students in the San Francisco immersion programs. Kelly is a 4th-grader whose Chinese American family has assimilated to the point that the children have lost their native language. Her parents enroll her in an immersion program so that she can converse with her grandmother, who speaks only Cantonese. The mother of Durell, an African American first grader, marvels at his ability to have a conversation with an older Chinese woman in a department store. It's a powerful piece, and provides a clear, urgent answer to the question it poses at the outset: "What does it mean to be an educated person in America today?"

* * *

So, the good news is that all is not grim. We can find hope and inspiration in corners of our educational universe where the democratic ideal is alive and, if not completely well, at least still kicking. But these examples should also be a call to action, an alarm that will shake us out of our collective complacency and remind us of what is possible. The road we've been on for the past decade is not the road we have to take going forward. But to change course, we have to reclaim something that every kindergartner brings with her to school: the ability to imagine. We have to push ourselves to see beyond the limitations of the here and now. We have to exercise what Myles Horton called the two-eyed theory: One eye on things as they are, the other on things as they could be.

In some ways, this is a rare moment. While education reform has gone through countless cycles throughout the past century, our schools have rarely been as much a part of the public conversation as they are today. From the popular documentaries *Waiting for Superman* and *Race to Nowhere* to NBC's *Education Nation* series to the Huffington Post's dedicated education page, teaching and learning are spending extended time on the mainstream media's front burner. The trouble is, all too often the messages that come through seem to be processed through the corporate-reform public relations machine. What classroom teacher can forget *Newsweek*'s March 2010 cover? "The key to saving American education," read the headline in block letters. Behind it, written over and over on a chalkboard, were the words, "We must fire bad teachers."[30]

If we're to believe *Waiting for Superman*, which tapped into the zeitgeist of the popular culture in ways no other film on education has, maybe it really is that easy. As the film ends, phrases crawl slowly across the screen: "The problems are complex. But the solution is simple. We know what to do."

Yet I don't know one person who spends their days in a city school—not one teacher, or student, or counselor, or teacher's aide, or social worker, or principal—who believes the solution to their educational challenges is simple. *Waiting for Superman* suggests that the answer, in large part, lies with the charter school movement. But several studies[31] have found that charters, on the whole, are no more effective than regular public schools. Besides, if, as the film argues, a big part of what makes charter schools so successful is increased freedom and the absence of directives from their districts, why should that lead to the conclusion that we need more charters? Instead, how about giving neighborhood schools what charters have: fewer restrictions, fewer mandates, more autonomy to work in ways that would best meet the needs of their students. Even that wouldn't be a "solution" for all that ails our schools. But it would be a welcome step.

Another would be for those on all sides of the current debates to engage in more genuine and wide-ranging conversations about what we really want from our schools, what education in a democracy should mean. The public dialogue is too often not a dialogue at all, but a clatter of simultaneous monologues—lots of noise and far too many snide remarks.

I know I've been guilty of participating this way at times. But in moments of greater clarity, I'm convinced that we'd all do well to spend more time truly listening to those we think we oppose, and asking tougher questions of ourselves and our allies. Is there any common ground upon which to build? Is there anything we ourselves need to rethink or reconsider? Is it possible to acknowledge that even those with whom we fiercely disagree are also committed to improving education for all children?

Naturalist and environmental activist Terry Tempest Williams[32] writes that the human heart "is the first home of democracy." It is, she says, "where we embrace our questions."

> Can we be equitable? Can we be generous? Can we listen with our whole beings, not just our minds, and offer our attention rather than our opinion? And do we have enough resolve in our hearts to act courageously, relentlessly, without giving up, trusting our fellow citizens to join us in our determined pursuit of a living democracy?[33]

Our hearts, our whole beings, too often tend to be disregarded in the public conversation about schools and what's best for children. Everything is intellectualized, and some would say that's as it should be. But maybe that's why many teachers feel so overwhelmed, even paralyzed, by the last decade's seismic shift toward test-centric, data-driven education. Good teachers know that much of their work is about connecting to the hearts and creative spirits of children, not just their minds. But the policies that direct and constrain their efforts insist otherwise.

The current taken-for-granted equation—that great test scores = great schools = a great education—has become an unchallenged starting point for any conversation about schooling in the United States. But it is a formula unbefitting a healthy democracy. For democracy to flourish, children need opportunities to exchange ideas freely, to discuss and debate, to puzzle through problems, to see the world through different lenses, to participate meaningfully in the life of their communities, to imagine—and work toward—a more just society.

The goals of schooling in a democracy are—or at least should be—expansive, inclusive, and full of hope. They defy the measure of any test.

Notes

Introduction

1. Barkan, 2011.
2. Machado, 1912/2007.
3. The single exception to this is "Juan at 16," which was written in 1999.
4. Rawls, 1971.

Chapter 1

1. Haberman, 1996.
2. Ayers, 2010.
3. Lorde, 1999.

Chapter 2

1. Strauss, 2001.
2. Hartocollis, 2001.
3. Finn, 2001.
4. Simon, 1997.
5. *Rethinking Schools*, 2000.

Chapter 3

1. Brockway et al., 2006.
2. Boden et al., 2006.
3. Gatto, 1990.
4. Arnal et al., 2008.
5. Bruckheimer et al., 1995.
6. Schachter, 2001.
7. Baldwin, 1996.

Chapter 4

1. Haberman, 1995.

Chapter 5

1. Freire, 1970.
2. Ibid., p. 71.
3. Delpit, 1995.
4. Irvine, p. 78.
5. Banks et al., 2005.
6. Delpit, 1995, p. 21.
7. Ibid., p. 45.
8. Howard, 2005.
9. Davis, 2003.
10. See Howard, 2005.
11. See Ayers, 2004.
12. Michie, 2009.
13. Ibid., p. 97.
14. Valenzuela, 1999, p. 265.
15. Wink, 2010.
16. Bartolome, 1996.
17. See Villegas & Lucas, 2002.
18. Ladson-Billings, 2002.
19. Delpit, 1995, pp. 46–47.

Chapter 6

1. Merton, 1966.

Chapter 8

1. The names of all students in Chapters 8–11 have been changed.

Chapter 10

1. Allensworth, 2005.
2. Orfield, Losen, Wald, & Swanson, 2004.
3. Ibid., p. 15.
4. See "Ground Zero" in this volume.
5. Meier, 2000.
6. Noguera, 2004.
7. Ibid., p. 29.
8. Rubinson, 2004, p. 58.
9. Fine, 2000, p. 177.
10. Brooks, 1999, p. 66.

11. See Seeley & MacGillivary, 2006.

12. See Martin & Halperin, 2006.

13. Lehr & Lange, 2003.

14. Martin & Halperin, 2006, p. 7.

Chapter 11

1. Allensworth, 2006.

2. Michie, 2005.

3. Ibid.

4. See Feagin, Vera, & Imani, 2004.

5. See Kivel, 2002.

6. We conducted eighteen interviews during the 2007–8 and 2008–9 academic years. Four were conducted by one of us, and fourteen by undergraduate students of color who assisted us with the project.

7. See Pierce, 1969 & 1995.

8. Solorzano, Ceja, & Yasso, 2000.

Chapter 12

1. Banchero, 2004.

2. *Chicago Tribune* Editorial Board, 2004.

3. Rodkin & Rainey, 2006.

4. Wilson, 2011.

5. Zinn, 2003, p. 8.

Chapter 14

1. Gates, 2011.

2. Chilcott et al., 2010.

3. Herbert, 2011.

4. Ibid.

5. Ripley, 2008.

6. From a talk at the TED conference, 2006.

Chapter 15

1. McKinley, 2010.

2. Posted on Jim Horn's "Schools Matter" blog, www.schoolsmatter.info, June 28, 2011.

3. Darling-Hammond, 2011.

4. See Barkan, 2011.

5. Cookson & Berger, 2003.
6. Ibid., p. 144.
7. Rose, 2009.
8. Fish, 2011.
9. Karp, 2008.
10. Obama, 2009.
11. Ravitch, 2009.
12. Personal communication, 2011.
13. See Luppescu et al., 2011.
14. Lipman, 2004.
15. Westheimer & Kahne, 2004.
16. Ibid., p. 239.
17. Ibid., p. 243.
18. Ibid., p. 244.
19. Ibid., p. 242.
20. Forum for Education and Democracy, 2008a, p. 11.
21. Personal communication, 2006.
22. Greene, 1997.
23. Obejas, 2011.
24. Peterson, 2005.
25. Chicago Grassroots Curriculum Taskforce, 2011.
26. Forum for Education and Democracy, 2008b.
27. Obama, 2011.
28. See the NNER website, http://www.nnerpartnerships.org/index.html.
29. Schneider & Jarmel, 2010.
30. *Newsweek*, March 15, 2010.
31. See Center for Research on Education Outcomes, 2009; Gleason, Clark, Tuttle, & Dwoyer, 2010.
32. Williams, 2004.
33. Ibid., pp. 83–84.

References

Allensworth, E. M. (2005). *Graduation and dropout trends in Chicago: A look at cohorts of students from 1991 to 2004.* Chicago: Consortium on Chicago School Research.

Allensworth, E. M. (2006). *Update to: From high school to the future: A first look at Chicago Public School graduates' college enrollment, college preparation, and graduation from four-year colleges.* Chicago: Consortium on Chicago School Research.

Arnal, S., et al. (Producers), & Cantet, L. (Director). (2008). *Entre les murs (The Class)* [Motion picture]. France: Haut et Court.

Ayers, W. (2004). Where we might begin with teaching. In K. D. Salas, et al. (Eds.), *The new teacher book. Finding purpose, balance, and hope during your first years in the classroom* (pp. 20–25). Milwaukee: Rethinking Schools.

Ayers, W. (2010). *To teach: The journey of a teacher* (3rd edition). New York: Teachers College Press.

Baldwin, J. (1996). A talk to teachers. In W. Ayers & P. Ford (Eds.), *City kids, city teachers: Reports from the front row* (pp. 219–227). New York: The New Press.

Banchero, S. (2004, July 18). One girl's struggle to find a future. *Chicago Tribune.* Retrieved from http://www.chicagotribune.com/news/watchdog/chi -040718nclb1-story,0,6822917,full.story

Banks, J., et al. (2005). Teaching diverse learners. In L. Darling-Hammond & J. Bransford (Eds.), *Preparing teachers for a changing world: What teachers should learn and be able to do* (pp. 232–274). San Francisco: Jossey-Bass.

Barkan, J. (2011). Got dough?: How billionaires rule our schools. *Dissent,* Winter 2011. Retrieved from http://www.dissentmagazine.org/article/?article=3781

Bartolomé, L. I. (1996). Beyond the methods fetish: Toward a humanizing pedagogy. In P. Leistyna, A. Woodrum, & S. A. Sherblom (Eds.), *Breaking free: The transformative power of critical pedagogy* (pp. 229–252). Cambridge, MA: Harvard Educational Review.

Boden, A., et al. (Producers), & Fleck, R. (Director). (2006). *Half nelson* [Motion picture]. United States: Hunting Lane Films.

Brockway, J., et al. (Producers), & Haines, R. (Director). *The Ron Clark story* [Motion picture]. United States/Canada: Alberta Film Entertainment/ Granada Entertainment.

Brooks, R. B. (1999). Creating a positive school climate: Strategies for fostering self-esteem, motivation, and resilience. In J. Cohen (Ed.), *Educating minds and hearts: Social emotional learning and the passage into adolescence* (pp. 61–73). New York: Teachers College Press.

Bruckheimer, J., et al. (Producers), & Smith, J. N. (Director). (1995). *Dangerous minds* [Motion picture]. United States: Hollywood Pictures.

Center for Research on Education Outcomes (2010). *Multiple choice: Charter performance in 16 states.* Stanford, CA: Author.

Chicago Grassroots Curriculum Taskforce (2011). *Revolutionizing education with grassroots curriculum* [Brochure]. Chicago: Author.

Chicago Tribune Editorial Board (2004, July 22). The tragedy of failed intentions. *Chicago Tribune.* Retrieved from http://articles.chicagotribune.com/2004-07-22/ news/0407220126_1_new-school-school-days-better-performing-schools

Chilcott, L., et al. (Producers), & Guggenheim, D. (Director). (2010). *Waiting for Superman* [Motion picture]. United States: Participant Media.

Cookson, P., & Berger, K. (2003). *Expect miracles: Charter schools and the politics of hope and despair.* Boulder, CO: Westview Press.

Darling-Hammond, L. (2011). The service of democratic education. *The Nation.* Retrieved from http://www.thenation.com/article/160850/ service-democratic-education

Davis, W. (2003). *Dreams from endangered cultures.* [Video file.] Retrieved from http://www.ted.com/talks/wade_davis_on_endangered_cultures.html

Delpit, L. (1995). *Other people's children: Cultural conflict in the classroom.* New York: The New Press.

Feagin, J. R., Vera, H., & Imani, N. (2004). Confronting White students: The Whiteness of university spaces. In A. Konradi & M. Schmidt (Eds.), *Reading between the lines: Toward an understanding of current social problems, 3rd edition* (pp. 456–467). Boston: McGraw-Hill.

Fine, M. (2000). A small price to pay for justice. In W. Ayers, M. Klonsky, & G. Lyon (Eds.), *A simple justice: The challenge of small schools* (pp. 168–179). New York: Teachers College Press.

Finn, C. (2001). Teaching patriotism: An education resource for Americans. *National Review Online.* Retrieved from http://old.nationalreview.com/com-ment/comment-finn120601.shtml

Fish, S. (2011, January 31). Race to the top of what? Obama on education. *The New York Times.* Retrieved from http://opinionator.blogs.nytimes.com/2011/01/31/race-to-the-top-of-what-obama-on-education/

Forum for Education and Democracy. (2008a). *Democracy at risk: The need for a new federal policy in education.* Stewart, OH: Author.

Forum for Education and Democracy. (2008b). What works: Teaching and learning. Retrieved from http://forumforeducation.org/our-issues/learning-teaching

Freire, P. (1970). *Pedagogy of the oppressed.* New York: Continuum.

Gates, B. (2011, February 28). How teacher development could revolutionize our schools. *The Washington Post.* Retrieved from http://www.washingtonpost.com/wp-dyn/content/article/2011/02/27/AR2011022702876.html

Gatto, J. T. (1990). Why schools don't educate. *The Sun,* June 1990. Retrieved from http://www.thesunmagazine.org/archives/937

Gleason, P., Clark, M., Tuttle, C. C., & Dwoyer, E. (2010). *The evaluation of charter school impacts: Final report.* Washington, D.C.: National Center for Education Evaluation and Regional Assistance.

Greene, M. (1997). Teaching as possibility: A light in dark times. *The Journal of Pedagogy, Pluralism, and Practice, 1*(1). Retrieved from http://www.lesley.edu/journals/jppp/1/jp3ii1.html

Haberman, M. (1995). *Star teachers of children in poverty.* Bloomington, IN: Kappa Delta Pi.

Haberman, M. (1996). The pedagogy of poverty versus good teaching. In W. Ayers & P. Ford (Eds.), *City kids, city teachers: Reports from the front row* (pp. 118–130). New York: The New Press.

Hartocollis, A. (2001, October 10). Lynne Cheney disputes official's call for more teaching of multiculturalism. *The New York Times.* Retrieved from http://www.nytimes.com/2001/10/10/nyregion/lynne-cheney-disputes-official-s-call-for-more-teaching-of-multiculturalism.html?src=pm

Herbert, B. (2011, March 25). Losing our way. *The New York Times.* Retrieved from http://www.nytimes.com/2011/03/26/opinion/26herbert.html

Howard, G. (2005). *We can't teach what we don't know: White teachers, multiracial schools,* 2nd edition. New York: Teachers College Press.

Irvine, J. J. (2003). *Educating teachers for diversity: Seeing with a cultural eye.* New York: Teachers College Press.

Karp, S. (2008). NCLB's selective vision of equality: Some gaps count more than others. In W. Ayers, G. Ladson-Billings, G. Michie, & P. Noguera, *City kids, city schools: More reports from the front row* (pp. 219–226). New York: The New Press.

Kivel, P. (2002). *Uprooting racism: How White people can work for racial justice.* New Society Publishers: Gabriola Island, British Columbia.

Ladson-Billings, G. (2002). "I ain't writin' nuttin' ": Permissions to fail and demands to succeed in urban classrooms. In L. Delpit & J. K. Dowdy (Eds.), *The skin that we speak: Thoughts on language and culture in the classroom* (pp. 107–120). New York: The New Press.

Lehr, C. A., & Lange, C. M. (2003). Alternative schools serving students with and without disabilities: What are the current issues and challenges? *Preventing School Failure*, 47(2), 59–65.

Lipman, P. (2004). *High stakes education: Inequality, globalization, and urban school reform*. New York: RoutledgeFalmer.

Lorde, A. (1999). A burst of light: Living with cancer. In J. Price & M. Shildrick (Eds.), *Feminist theory and the body: A reader* (pp. 149–162). New York: Routledge.

Luppescu, S., et al. (2011). *Three eras of Chicago school reform*. Chicago: Consortium on Chicago School Research.

Machado, A. (1912/2007). *Campos de castilla*. Mineola, NY: Dover Publications.

Martin, N., & Halperin, S. (2006). *Whatever it takes: How twelve communities are reconnecting out-of-school youth*. Washington, DC: American Youth Policy Forum.

McKinley, J. (2010, March 12). Texas conservatives win curriculum change. *The New York Times*. Retrieved from http://www.nytimes.com/2010/03/13/education/13texas.html

Meier, D. (2000). The crisis of relationships. In W. Ayers, M. Klonsky, & G. Lyon (Eds.), *A simple justice: The challenge of small schools* (pp. 33–37). New York: Teachers College Press.

Merton, T. (1966). A letter to Jim Forest [dated February 21, 1966]. Reproduced in W. Shannon (Ed.), *The Hidden Ground of Love: Letters by Thomas Merton*. New York: Harcourt.

Michie, G. (2005). *See you when we get there: Teaching for change in urban schools*. New York: Teachers College Press.

Michie, G. (2009). *Holler if you hear me: The education of a teacher and his students*, 2nd edition. New York: Teachers College Press.

Noguera, P. (2004). Transforming high schools. *Educational Leadership*, 61(8), 26–31.

Obama, B. (2009, July 16). Remarks by the President to the NAACP Centennial Convention. Retrieved from http://blogs.suntimes.com/sweet/2009/07/obamas_naacp_speech.html

Obama, B. (2011, January 25). Remarks by the President in State of the Union Address. Retrieved from http://www.Whitehouse.gov/the-press-office/2011/01/25/remarks-president-state-union-address

Obejas, A. (2011, February 7). How (and why) those Rogers Park high schoolers made their anti-Rahm/pro-Miguel video. Retrieved from http://www.wbez.org/blog/achy-obejas/2011-02-07/how-and-why-those-rogers-park-high-schoolers-made-their-anti-rahmpro-mig

Orfield, G., Losen, D., Wald, J., & Swanson, C. (2004). *Losing our future: How minority youth are being left behind by the graduation rate crisis.* Cambridge, MA: The Civil Rights Project at Harvard University.

Peterson, B. (2005). Write the truth: Presidents and slaves. In E. Gutstein & B. Peterson (Eds.), *Rethinking mathematics: Teaching social justice by the numbers* (pp. 140–147). Milwaukee: Rethinking Schools.

Pierce, C. M. (1969). Is bigotry the basis of the medical problems in the ghetto? In J. C. Norman (Ed.), *Medicine in the ghetto* (pp. 301–312). New York: Meredith.

Pierce, C. M. (1995). Stress analogs of racism and sexism: Terrorism, torture, and disaster. In C. V. Willie, P. P. Rieker, B. M. Kramer, & B. S. Brown (Eds.), *Mental health, racism, and sexism* (pp. 277–293). Pittsburgh: University of Pittsburgh Press.

Ravitch, D. (2009, February 4). Is Arne Duncan really Margaret Spellings in drag? *Education Week.* Available at: http://blogs.edweek.org/edweek/Bridging-Differences/2009/02/is_arne_duncan_really_margaret.html

Rawls, J. (1971). *A theory of justice.* Cambridge, MA: Harvard University Press.

Rethinking Schools. (2000). Introduction to special issue on multicultural education. *Rethinking Schools,* 15(1). Available at: http://www.rethinkingschools.org/archive/15_01/Rsmu151.shtml

Ripley A. (2008, November 26). Rhee tackles classroom challenge. *Time.* Retrieved from http://www.time.com/time/magazine/article/0,9171,1862444,00.html

Robinson, K. (2007). *Ken Robinson says schools kill creativity.* [Video file.] Retrieved from http://www.ted.com/talks/ken_robinson_says_schools_kill_creativity.html.

Rodkin, D., & Rainey, A. (2006, October). The A+ team. *Chicago Magazine.* Retrieved from http://www.chicagomag.com/Chicago-Magazine/October-2006/The-A-Team/

Rose, M. (2009). *Why school?: Reclaiming education for all of us.* New York: The New Press.

Rubinson, F. (2004). Urban dropouts: Why so many and what can be done? In S. R. Steinberg & J. L. Kincheloe (Eds.), *19 urban questions: Teaching in the city* (pp. 53–67). New York: Peter Lang.

Schachter, J. (Producer), & Guggenhiem, D. (Director). (2001). *The first year* [Motion picture]. United States: Public Broadcasting Service.

Schneider, K. (Producer), & Jarmel, M. (Director). (2010). *Speaking in tongues* [Motion picture]. United States: PatchWorks Films.

Seeley, K., & MacGillivary, H. (2006). *School policies that engage students and families.* Denver, CO: National Center for School Engagement. Retrieved from http://www.schoolengagement.org/TruancypreventionRegistry/Admin/Resources/Resources/SchoolPoliciesthatEngageStudentsandFamilies.pdf

Simon, L. A. & Trench, T. (Producers), & Simon, L. A. (Director). (1997). *Fear and learning at Hoover Elementary* [Motion Picture]. United States: Josepha Producciones.

Smith, W. A., Allen, W. R., & Danley, L. L. (2007). "Assume the position . . . you fit the description": Psychosocial experiences and racial battle fatigue among African American male college students. *American Behavioral Scientist*, 51(4), 551–578.

Solorzano, D., Ceja, M., & Yasso, T. (2000). Critical race theory, racial microaggressions, and campus racial climate: The experiences of African American college students. *The Journal of Negro Education*, 69 (1/2), 60–73.

Strauss, V. (2001, September 30). Sept. 11 prompts lesson review; Educators rethink multiculturalism. *The Washington Post*, p. B1.

Valenzuela, A. (1999). *Subtractive schooling: U.S.-Mexican youth and the politics of caring*. Albany: State University of New York Press.

Villegas, A. M., & Lucas, T. (2002). *Educating culturally responsive teachers: A coherent approach*. Albany, NY: SUNY Press.

Westheimer, J., & Kahne, J. (2004). What kind of citizen? The politics of educating for democracy. *American Educational Research Journal*, 41(2), 237–269.

Williams, T. T. (2004). *The open spaces of democracy*. Barrington, MA: The Orion Society.

Wilson, B. (2011, January). The mom brigade. *Chicago Magazine*, pp. 54–62.

Wink, J. (2010). *Critical pedagogy: Notes from the real world*. New York: Prentice Hall.

Zinn, H. (2003). *A people's history of the United States: 1492–present*. New York: Harper Perennial.

Index

About the Author

Gregory Michie has worked in Chicago schools and communities for over 20 years, including 9 years as a classroom teacher. He has also taught video production and media literacy in after-school programs, volunteered with young men in gangs, and worked for the past decade as a teacher educator in the city. His teaching memoir *Holler If You Hear Me* is widely used in teacher preparation programs across the country. He currently teaches 7th and 8th graders in a Chicago public school, and is a senior research associate at Concordia University Chicago's Center for Policy Studies and Social Justice.